Physical Characteristics of the Chow Chow

(from the American Kennel Club breed standard)

Topline: Straight, strong and level from the withers to the root of the tail.

Body: Short, compact, close coupled, strongly muscled, broad, deep and well let down in the flank. The body, back, coupling and croup must all be short to give the required square build.

Hindquarters: The rear assembly broad, powerful, and well muscled in the hips and thighs, heavy in bone with rear and front bone approximately equal. Stifle joint shows little angulation, is well knit and stable. Hock joint well let down and appears almost straight.

Tail: Set high and carried closely to the back at all times, following the line of the spine at the start.

Coat: There are two types of coat; rough and smooth. Both are double coated. In the rough coat, the outer coat is abundant, dense, straight and offstanding, rather coarse in texture; the undercoat soft, thick and wooly. The coat forms a profuse ruff around the head and neck, framing the head. Tail well feathered.

Color: Clear colored, solid or solid with lighter shadings in the ruff, tail and featherings. There are five colors in the Chow: red (light golden to deep mahogany), black, blue, cinnamon (light fawn to deep cinnamon) and cream.

Feet: Round, compact, catlike, standing well up on the thick toe pads.

Size: The average height of adult specimens is 17 to 20 inches at the withers.

Chow Chow

◇

by Richard G. Beauchamp

Contents

KENNEL CLUB BOOKS® CHOW CHOW

ISBN 13: 978-1-59378-260-3

Copyright © 2005 • Kennel Club Books® • A Division of BowTie, Inc.
40 Broad Street, Freehold, New Jersey 07728 USA
Cover Design Patented: US 6,435,559 B2 • Printed in South Korea

Photography by Carol Ann Johnson
with additional photographs by

Ashbey Studios, Paulette Braun, Bernd Brinkmann, T.J. Calhoun, Alan and Sandy Carey, Carolina Biological Supply, Isabelle Français, Carol Ann Johnson, Bill Jonas, Alice van Kempen, Kohler Photography, Dr. Dennis Kunkel, Tam C. Nguyen, Antonio Philippe, Perry Phillips, Phototake, Jean Claude Revy, Alice Roche and C. James Webb.

Illustrations by Renée Low and Patricia Peters.

The publisher wishes to thank all of the owners whose dogs are illustrated in this book, including Linda Albert, Barbara Bakert, George and Kathy Beliew, Ernie Coy, Wayne and Lynda Eyster, Pat Rose and Karen Tracy.

One of China's legendary dogs, the Chow Chow has been used for hunting, caravan guarding, sampan and junk guarding and for food. It is also a superior pet for the right owner, though it has never achieved pet status in China.

HISTORY OF THE

CHOW CHOW

The romantic tales surrounding the origin of the beautiful and temperamentally unique Chow Chow are countless. The somewhat blurred origins and unusual looks of this breed have led to legendary and fanciful links to all kinds of animals outside the canine world. Not the least of these legends is the one that claims it is the bear rather than the wolf from which the Chow descends.

There is nothing to substantiate the Chow's relationship to the bear, but those who choose to believe this cite many characteristics that the breed shares with no other animal but the bear. Supporters of this theory claim that a form of primitive wild animal, which is now extinct, is the ancestor of the Chow.

All other dogs are known to have descended from the progenitors of the wolf. This, according to the bear theorists, explains why most other dogs either look away from the Chow Chow at first meeting or immediately prepare themselves to attack.

When one stops to consider the bear's independent nature, its blue tongue and the stilted manner in which it walks—all characteristics of the Chow Chow—it becomes understandable how the theory took root. There is also the remarkable resemblance of the bear cub to the Chow. If nothing else, all this makes one wonder if Mother Nature just might have lent some ironic twist to the evolution of the Chow.

Although China embraces the Chow Chow as one of its own, historical documents originating in China consistently refer to the breed as "the foreign Chow." This substantiates the more scientific research that reveals the Chow was of Arctic origin, migrating to China with the barbarian tribes that frequently invaded China in the 11th century BC.

These barbarian invaders had dogs of formidable size that were described as having black tongues and being so fierce that they could easily bring down humans as if they were straws. These warrior dogs sometimes resembled lions in color as well as in their head

CANIS LUPUS

"Grandma, what big teeth you have!" The gray wolf, a familiar figure in fairy tales and legends, has had its reputation tarnished and its population pummeled over the centuries. Yet it is the descendants of this much-feared creature to which we open our homes and hearts. Our beloved dog, *Canis domesticus*, derives directly from the gray wolf, a highly social canine that lives in elaborately structured packs. In the wild, the gray wolf can range from 60 to 175 pounds, standing between 25 and 40 inches in height.

characteristics. They also had long claws and shaggy manes that covered their necks.

Though the Chow's long existence in China can be traced through its image on bronzes and in paintings, much of the breed's documented history was destroyed by the Emperor Chin Shih, who wantonly destroyed most of China's literature in 225 BC. The records that did survive add some interesting details to the earlier descriptions of the warrior dogs.

These writings describe the dogs as being completely different from other breeds of dog with large broad heads, short muzzles and small eyes. The lips are described as not overlapping but just touching, giving them a unique aloof expression.

It appears that although these warrior dogs were devoted to their keepers, they were extremely hostile to strangers. Their fierce natures made them ideal candidates for their roles as war dogs. It is interesting to note that these same dogs proved to be excellent hunters and herding dogs.

As centuries passed, the breed's fierce nature mellowed and the dogs could be assigned duties of a more domestic nature: draft dog, hunter, herder, guardian of the home and, unfortunately for the dogs, as food for the family as well.

The Chinese (and subsequent English) slang word for something edible is "chow." The dogs kept for this purpose were considered a great delicacy. Thus, dog meat was sold and eaten throughout China and Korea until it was prohibited by law in China in 1915.

Chinese legend gives us purely practical reasons for two of the Chow's most distinguishing characteristics: the straighter the hind leg, the more abundant the meat; and the bluer the tongue, the more tender and delicious the meat.

WEST MEETS EAST

There can be no doubt that as the first clipper ships entered Chinese harbors, British sailors were fascinated by the multitude of curiosities this strange country afforded. Certainly not the least of these oddities was this dog that was more bear- or lion-like than anything ever seen by British seamen. It is little wonder the sailors took their canine curiosities back to England with them on return voyages. In 1780 the first Chows arrived in Great Britain.

Little is known of the fate of those first exotic immigrants to England. It was not until 1840 that a newspaper account tells of several Chows who were kept in the London Zoological Park. They were referred to as the "wild dog of China."

In 1880, however, records document the exhibition of Chinese Puzzle, a black Chow

At the turn of the 20th century, China was exporting short-coated Chows. They were called edible dogs and according to customs forms they were considered food animals like swine, chickens and ducks.

female imported directly from China. Chinese Puzzle was shown at a dog show that took place at the famous Crystal Palace in London. Evidently the look of Chinese Puzzle caught the eye

PURE-BRED PURPOSE

Given the vast range of the world's 400 or so pure breeds of dog, it's fair to say that domestic dogs are the most versatile animal in the kingdom. From the tiny 1-pound lap dog to the 200-pound guard dog, dogs have adapted to every need and whim of their human masters. Humans have selectively bred dogs to alter physical attributes like size, color, leg length, mass and skull diameter in order to suit our own needs and fancies. Dogs serve humans not only as companions and guardians but also as hunters, exterminators, shepherds, rescuers, messengers, warriors, babysitters and more!

The Chinese Foo Dog is suspected of being a direct relative of the Chow Chow.

Author Richard G. Beauchamp, long-time Chow fancier, judge and breeder, pictured here with one of his favorite Chows.

and captured the fancy of some of London's most fashionable ladies, including the Marchioness of Huntley.

When the Marchioness was offered a Chow that her relative, the Earl of Lonsdale, had brought back from China, she not only accepted the gift but immediately requested the Earl bring back more of the dogs on his next trip. Upon the arrival of the new dogs, Lady Huntley set about breeding Chows, heading up the kennel with an imported male she named Periodot.

A Periodot daughter, Periodot II, bred by the Marchioness was subsequently sold to Lady Granville Gordon, who established a highly respected breeding kennel on the blood of this female. Lady Gordon's daughter, Lady Faudel-Phillips, shared her interest in the Chow Chow and became the most important and influential breeder in England. The Ladies Gordon and Phillips

Lady Faudel-Phillips, circa 1932, with one of her Amwell Chows. The Amwell kennels produced many champion Chows.

were to produce the first English-bred champion Chow, who was named simply Blue Blood.

The National Chow Chow Club of Great Britain (NCCCGB) was formed in 1895 and an official standard of the breed was drawn up at the first meeting. The club's first show for the breed was held at Westminster in the same year. It is interesting to note that the same standard, with only minor adjustments, continues to exist to this day and has been used as a basis for practically every other standard around the world.

By December of that same year, the NCCCGB was able to stage its first show and no less than 54 Chows were entered. The impressive turnout of dogs was the talk of the dog fancy and

EARLY CANINE GROUPS

As early as the first century AD, Romans had classified dogs into six general groups: House Guardian Dogs, Shepherd Dogs, Sporting Dogs, War Dogs, Scent Dogs and Sight Dogs. Most dogs we know today can trace their ancestry directly back to dogs from these groups. Many other breeds were developed by combining two or more individuals from those original groups to create yet another "breed."

helped the breed secure a position of respect among die-hard dog fanciers throughout the country.

When Lady Gordon died, her daughter Lady Phillips fell heir to all of the Chows. With these dogs and some of her own, Lady

Phillips established the legendary Amwell Chow Chow Kennel in 1919. The kennel was to remain in operation until Lady Phillips's death in 1943.

With the breed in the hands of England's wealthy and titled men and women, the Chow Chow flourished. The breed's fanciers could well afford huge kennels and the talented stockmen it took to manage them. The breed grew in number and in quality.

The first Chow Chow to become an English champion was an import, Ch. Chow VIII, which was described as a dog of good type though somewhat lacking in coat. Unfortunately Chow VIII had a temperament that left much to be desired. Though his nasty tempera-

A British dog breeder, Miss Joshua, was famed for the beautiful expressive faces of her dogs. The Chow look has been described as "scowling" but many observers describe the breed as leonine, or lion-like.

Mrs. Scaramanga's champion Chows were painted by Maud Earl in the 1930s.

ment resulted in frequent changes of ownership, it barely affected Chow VIII's show career, which was somewhat spectacular for the day. Temperament notwithstanding, it is believed England's standard of the breed was written with Chow VIII as its model.

As years progressed, word of these mighty and exotic dogs spread to Europe and to America. In Europe it became a mark of distinction among the wealthy to own one of the edible wild dogs of China. While high prices were paid for the dogs in Europe, the breed was not really accepted by serious dog fanciers there until many years later.

In England the Chow Chow was forced to survive the devastating effects of two World Wars. With the determination so typical of the English, fanciers not only

helped the breed inch forward through the worst of times but actually brought the breed to a resplendent level of quality shortly after World War II. There can be no doubt the breed owes its celebrated status throughout the world to England and the great dog men

TWO FAMOUS CHOONAM CHOWS

Eng. Ch. Choonam Hung Kwong was the first of his breed to win Best in Show at Crufts Dog Show. He created a minor sensation, as he was described as "a magnificent specimen...arrogant and proud, with great presence."

Eng. Ch. Choonam Brilliantine was sold to America in 1925 for the then fantastic sum of £1800. At that time a modest house could have been purchased in England for half that amount.

In an illustration dated 1934, Vere Temple captured the antics of grandfather Chow looking over a litter only a few weeks old.

and women who embraced the "edible wild dog of China" and shaped it into the loved and respected breed it is today.

THE CHOW CHOW IN THE UNITED STATES

As the Chow Chow breed grew in number and quality in Great Britain, the breed was attracting a mighty following in North America as well. The first Chow to be exhibited in the United States appears in the 1890 catalog of the Westminster Kennel Club. In 1905 Mrs. Charles E. Proctor founded her Blue Dragon Kennels, and in that same year Mrs. Proctor imported Chinese Chum, destined to become America's first champion Chow. Veterans of the breed consider Ch. Chinese Chum to be the cornerstone of the breed in the US. Dr. and Mrs. Henry Jarrett had also established a kennel in Philadelphia and campaigned their

In 1933 this Chow, Eng. Ch. Rochow Dragoon, held the record of winning 31 Challenge Certificates. He was famed for his cat-like feet and bold body, to say nothing of his other outstanding characteristics.

dogs throughout the East. In 1906 the Jarretts were instrumental in founding the Chow Chow Club, Inc., the parent club of the breed.

World War I had a decidedly negative effect upon dog shows and dog breeding in North America, though not as harsh as its

Eng. Ch. Choonam Moonbeam and Ch. Choonam Chang Li are fine examples of Mrs. V. A. Manoch's Choonam Kennel, which was famous in the 1930s for its very high prices and very high-quality Chows.

A head study of Eng. Ch. Rochow Dragoon, the world's greatest Chow champion of his time. His head exhibits all of what is desired in the breed: the full ruff, the "scowl" and the overall leonine look.

effect in Europe. While enthusiasts maintained their devotion to the breed, activity came to a near standstill. In the 1920s, however, there was a marked acceleration of interest in the breed. This popularity was undoubtedly due in a great part to the fact that a Chow Chow was living in the White House with President Calvin Coolidge. Unfortunately this upsurge in popularity proved disastrous to the character and the image of the breed. The Chow market was flooded with ill-bred and ill-tempered stock bred by unscrupulous individuals capitalizing on the demand for puppies. Soon the breed was overcome by nasty-spirited dogs earning the Chow a reputation as not only untrustworthy but in some cases

downright dangerous. Those who truly loved the breed were left to live down this damaged reputation and reeducate the general public as to how great a companion a well-bred Chow could be.

Without a doubt, the charismatic Ch. Yang Fu Tang, a great winner in the 1930s, helped to heal the damage done to the breed's reputation with his winning ways. His son won the Non-Sporting Group at the famous Westminster dog show in 1940. No other Chow would win a Group at Westminster until 1969, when the red male Ch. Gotschall's Van Van did so under the esteemed all-breed judge Alva Rosenberg.

It is to the credit of Chow Chow breeders and fanciers of the latter half of the 20th century throughout America that great

This Egyptian pottery piece from thousands of years ago shows a resemblance to the Chow. A noted similarity is the carriage of the tail curved over the back.

emphasis was placed upon the temperament and image of the breed. Diehards of the breed throughout the US made great strides in these areas. Certainly particular credit must be given to Raymond and Valetta Gotschall (Gotschall), Joel Marston (Starcrest), Dr. Samuel Draper (Liontamer) and Pete and Howard Kendall (Poppyland). These individuals bred dogs that were not only of superior type but also blessed with exemplary temperaments. Popular judge and author, Draper did much to change the breed's reputation through his breeding program and his popular books on the Chow. Dogs bred and campaigned by Liontamer Chows possessed ideal people-loving temperaments as well as proper gait, construction and coat quality.

Other standouts in the Chow Chow world in that period were Leroy and Georgia King (Kinghai) and Cliff and Vivian Shryock. The Shryocks added considerably to the breed's reputation by importing Ch. Ghat de a Moulaine from France and English, American, Mexican and Canadian Ch. Ukwong Fleur from England. Another Chow Chow mainstay has been Dr. Joanne Schmidt O'Brien, whose parents owned Linnchow Kennels in Tinley Park, Illinois in the 1930s and '40s. Dr. O'Brien has maintained the family interest in Chow Chows well over half a century. In fact, the author took great pleasure in awarding Dr. O'Brien's Linnchow Charlie Brown Best of Breed from the classes and then Non-Sporting Group First at the Trillium Dog Fanciers show in Toronto, Canada as recently as November 2, 2002.

California has long been a Chow Chow haven, and the dogs produced by Bob and Love Banghart (Rebelrun) and George and Kathy Belieu (Imagine) have made their mark nationwide. The outstanding dogs produced by these two kennels have garnered magnificent records including countless Breed, Group and all-breed Best in Show awards.

The Chow Chow of today has risen above its unattractive reputation of the past and stands proudly among man's most popular and devoted companions. For the person who takes the time to understand the character of the Chow Chow, there can be no greater canine friend.

This 1934 series of drawings and captions shows those faults of the Chow that were of most concern to dog judges.

Incorrect back leg.
Angular hock.
Tail set too low.

Too low on leg.
Down on pasterns.
Harefeet; pointed and narrow.

Tucked up.
(Upward slope of ventral line.)
Tail falling to one side.

Narrow chest.

Pointed muzzle.

Eyes too round.
Large ears, too narrowly set.

"Chippendale" legs.

Out at shoulder.

Too high on leg.

Narrow chested.
(as made to stand in ring).

CHARACTERISTICS OF THE
CHOW CHOW

Intrigued by the exotic history of the Chow Chow? Enchanted by the roly-poly bear cub appearance of a Chow puppy? You aren't alone! In fact, those two things alone have caused the Chow Chow to soar to heights of popularity on more than one occasion in the breed's history, but unfortunately it was to the detriment of the breed. Unscrupulous buyers rushed forth to capitalize on demand for the breed, and bad temperaments were ignored.

A Chow Chow is an absolutely wonderful breed—for the right person! Before dashing out to buy a Chow—in fact before thinking about buying any dog—a person should definitely sit down and think the prospect out thoroughly. Teddy-bear-like Chow puppies snuggled together fast asleep one on top of the other are absolutely irresistible, I assure you. Chow puppies' attractiveness as a subject for photography puts them on calendars and greetings cards around the world. This is a good part of what encourages well-meaning but misguided individuals to dash out to buy a Chow puppy for themselves or as a gift for someone they know who "should have" a dog.

This is not to say the pudgy little ball of fluff you bring home will not be as cute and entertaining as those calendar pin-up pups. There is no doubt about that. However, calendars and greeting cards do not address the reality of dog ownership. Real Chow Chow puppies spend their days investigating, digging, chewing, eating, relieving themselves, having tummy aches and needing trips to the veterinarian for inoculations and so many other minor problems.

Puppies don't come pre-educated. Everything that you

DESHELLING THE CHOW
Chow Chows are perfectly content to live their lives out with the person or people in their own household and have no real need for attention from others. However, Chow Chows that are not given proper socialization can become introverted and sullen, often cross, with people whom they do not know.

Young people are attracted to puppies perhaps even more than adults are, but not every youngster is willing or able to be a responsible caregiver.

However, all too often it is your spouse, your mother or father or anyone living in your home who will also share the responsibility of caring for the dog. The Chow Chow must be welcomed and wanted by all members of your household, or it will become a burden to all.

Mothers seem to fall into this role naturally—not necessarily because they want to, but the mothers I know are not inclined to stand by and watch any creature be neglected. Thus it is "mom" who takes the dog to the vet, who rushes out to buy the dog food and who takes the dog out for a walk. Mom just may not want any more duties than she already has!

Children will promise just about anything in order to get a puppy, but the question that has to be addressed seriously is what will happen after the novelty of owning a new dog has worn off. Again, who will ultimately be responsible for the dog's care?

Even if the entire family thinks a dog would be a great idea, does the lifestyle and schedule of the household lend itself to the demands of proper dog care? Someone must always be available to see to a dog's basic needs: feeding, exercise, coat care, access to the outdoors when required, and so on. If you or your family are gone from morning to night or if you travel frequently and are

think a well-behaved dog should know how to do will have to be taught. Chows learn quickly, but that is not to say they may feel it is entirely necessary to respond to your request. It takes time and patience to get through to a Chow, and the question you must ask yourself is whether or not you have the time and patience to do this educating.

WHO WINS THE PRIZE?
Who will ultimately be responsible for the dog's day-to-day care? Does that individual really want a dog? If you are the only person who needs to answer that question, there is no problem.

away from home for long periods of time, the dog still must be cared for. Will someone willingly be present to do so? Are you prepared to pay the costs of frequent boarding at a kennel while you are gone?

You must also stop to think about the suitability of the breed for the household, whether household means half a dozen children and adults or just you. Very young children can be rough and unintentionally hurt a puppy by dropping, pulling at or hitting it. It also takes a lot of talking to convince a toddler that a Chow's tail is not a handle to be pulled. No self-respecting Chow Chow is going to enjoy that, nor should it be expected to. Chows are not blessed with the tolerance of a Labrador Retriever or the pain-endurance of a Mastiff or Staffordshire.

On the other hand, as a tiny puppy grows into a large and enthusiastic young adult seemingly overnight, it can overwhelm and sometimes injure an infant or small child in an exuberant moment.

IS A CHOW THE RIGHT DOG FOR YOU?

The entire history of the Chow has been one of close association with people, but the breed has never been one that has had a need to lavish attention on the humans around him. The Chow

The Chow is not the dog for every family. Chow owners must, above all, be patient in raising and training their dogs.

Chow is inclined to be a one-person, or at best a one-family, kind of a dog. Visitors are fine but not necessary to a Chow's existence. They are homebodies who live to be with their owner. Not particularly in their owners' laps, mind you, but nearby—where they can make sure you don't get into trouble.

What kind of person should own a Chow? One word will describe the person—patient. If the Chow owner is patient, he will be rewarded with a life companion whose devotion knows no end and whose sense of humor knows no bounds.

Lady Dunbar of Mochrum, one of England's pioneer breeders of the Chow, described the breed as follows: "...The Chow has many noble qualities, his heart cannot be taken by storm, but, once given, it is yours forever..." Though written a hundred years ago, this description of the Chow's character remains as apt today as then.

I have owned many breeds of dog. None has been so independent, so humorous, so disdainful of strangers or absolutely devoted as the Chow. If molding a dog's spirit to conform to your picture of the ideal canine companion is an important factor in dog ownership, consider a breed other than the Chow. You can guide a Chow in the direction you want it to go, but you can't push it there. Nor can you be heavy-handed. As rough and tumble as the breed might be, as sturdy a constitution as the Chow might have and as high as its tolerance for discomfort might be, a Chow is completely incapable of withstanding being struck in anger. This devastates the Chow and, if subjected to treatment of this nature, it can turn even the most amiable youngster into a neurotic and unpredictable adult.

This is not to say the Chow owner needs to or should be passive in raising and training a Chow. On the contrary, a Chow must start understanding household rules from the first moment he comes into your home. What it will take to accomplish this is patience and a firm but gentle hand. This does not mean a stern reprimand or a resounding slap on the floor with a folded newspaper can never be administered. Somehow, even the youngest Chow understands the difference

Essentially a one-person (or one-family) dog, the Chow requires much human companionship and interaction with his owner.

between being corrected and being abused.

If your idea of keeping a dog is having it live outdoors with minimal owner interaction, please do not consider a Chow. The Chow must have constant human companionship and social interaction not only with its owner but also with all kinds of people and other dogs. The Chow raised without this socialization can easily become introverted and sullen. The young Chow can pass through an adolescent stage when it decides his owner or family is all that is necessary for his well-being and can become very anti-social unless made to understand this is unacceptable.

It is then up to the caring owner to help guide the Chow through this difficult stage. Patience, persistence and support will help your Chow through this

---

HEART-HEALTHY

In this modern age of ever-improving cardio-care, no doctor or scientist can dispute the advantages of owning a dog to lower a person's risk of heart disease. Studies have proven that petting a dog, walking a dog and grooming a dog all show positive results toward lowering your blood pressure. The simple routine of exercising your dog—going outside with the dog and walking, jogging or playing catch—is heart-healthy in and of itself. If you are normally less active than your physician thinks you should be, adopting a dog may be a smart option to improve your own quality of life as well as that of another creature.

TAMING AND TRAINING THE LION

If a dog that thrills to training or following routines is what you consider an ideal pet and companion, perhaps looking to a breed other than the Chow Chow would be a good idea. Chows are notoriously independent and are more likely to respond when they take the notion rather than to follow a command. Chows don't refuse to obey, but they will take their time in deciding just when the response should take place.

awkward time, but it does take time and a commitment to stay out there with the "bashful" youngster.

The Chow character is both unique and contradictory. The breed seems almost to come pre-housebroken. It is a lesson the breed seems to want to learn and once learned only a major catastrophe can get the adult to transgress. On the other hand, the breed has a stubborn streak a mile wide.

Anyone who has lived with a Chow knows how quickly the breed understands what you are trying to teach. The experienced owner also knows how long it can be before the Chow chooses to comply. Stubbornness extends itself to everything the Chow learns. Do everything you possibly can to avoid having your Chow develop bad habits, because once something is learned (good or bad), it takes practically an act of Congress before you will be able to convince your Chow to forget that habit.

Most Chows look at strangers on an impartial basis. Fine if their master decides to have friends come to call, just as fine if not. As indifferent as the Chow can be to the comings and goings of visitors, there is no indifference when it comes to an intruder! What appears to be the laziest Chow known to the free world can suddenly become a hurricane of protectiveness when someone tries to enter its premises without an invitation!

Then, too, Chows seem to make "blanket judgements." If your Chow sees the little boy next door as a kind and gentle play-mate, all little children will prob-ably be high on your Chow's list of favorite people. On the other hand, if the uniformed delivery man threatens or strikes your Chow, pity any other uniformed man who enters your premises! Make sure your Chow's initial introduction to people is a posi-tive experience. You will be hard pressed to change your Chow's mind once it is made up.

This applies to change in ownership as well. Some adult Chow Chows may rehome easily. Most do not. A good many breeds are just as happy living in one place as another, just so long as they are well fed and well treated. Not so with the Chow!

Does Chow ownership sound like a challenge? If so, you have definitely gotten my message. There is no doubt that a Chow will be able to test you in every way possible, but I am inclined to believe it is all done to determine whether or not you are worthy of being in the Chow's presence. If you do qualify, you will have a companion the likes of whom you will never forget.

The freshly bathed and groomed Chow in full coat certainly presents a beautiful picture, but a Chow enjoys digging holes and traipsing through mud puddles as much as any other dog. This requires bathing and grooming and yes, house cleaning, because Chows do molt—both coat types, Rough and Smooth.

Although Chows are not as gregari-ous as some breeds, they can befriend a fellow canine if properly introduced as puppies.

Although the Smooth Chow does not shed as abundantly as the Rough, there is still a lot of coat to contend with. This is a cream-colored Smooth Chow.

With time, practice, and the right grooming tools, you can keep your Chow always looking as though it just stepped out of the grooming parlor. Do note, however, that I did say with time, practice and the right grooming tools!

MALE OR FEMALE?

While some individuals may have their personal preferences for the sex of their dog, I can honestly say that both the male and the female Chows make wonderful companions. The decision will have more to do with the lifestyle and intentions of the owner than differences between the sexes. The male is larger, grander and sometimes a bit more aggressive. He's also much more heavily coated. The female is a bit smaller and usually carries less coat. Still, there are some very laid-back males and some bitches who are a bit more high-strung.

Spaying the female and neutering the male will not change the character of your pet but will avoid the problems you will have to contend with should you choose not to do so. Neutering also precludes the possibility of your pet adding to the extreme pet overpopulation problem that concerns environmentalists worldwide.

COAT TYPES

An important consideration that must be addressed is whether at

Grooming the Rough Chow will require considerable effort if you want your dog to look his absolute best.

least one of the Chow's owners is willing to assume the responsibility for coat care. To divide this responsibility among unwilling members of the family is sheer folly. The task will not be done well or, if it is done at all, not done properly.

As much as we admire the properly groomed Rough Chow's

crowning glory, one must be realistic and understand the coat looks that way only because it is given time and attention. Fortunately, Chow lovers who do not want the additional responsibility of the Rough's coat have the option of selecting a Smooth puppy or adult. In this case you have all the Chow benefits without the work that maintaining that beautiful coat entails.

HEALTH CONSIDERATIONS

In the wild any genetically transferred infirmity that would interfere with a newborn animal's survival would automatically be eliminated from the gene pool. Inability to nurse, to capture food as an adult and to escape from a predator are obviously impairments that would shorten an animal's life very quickly.

We who control the breeding of our domesticated dogs are intent upon saving all the puppies in a litter, but in preserving life we also perpetuate health problems. Our humanitarian proclivities thus have drawbacks as well.

Like all other breeds of domesticated dogs, Chows have their share of hereditary problems. As careful as long-time Chow breeders might be in the stock they choose for their breeding programs, hereditary problems still do crop up.

The following represent problems that exist in the breed. This

PUPPY SELECTION

In choosing a Chow Chow puppy, a happy, healthy and extroverted puppy is the bottom line. Never select the shy shrinking violet that cowers in a corner nor, on the other hand, the standoffish pup that growls or challenges a stranger. Both of these extremes can lead to problems in adulthood with which the average pet owner is not prepared to cope.

does not mean that the puppy you buy or the line from which it comes will necessarily be afflicted

The best exercise for a Chow Chow is that which lets him spend time with his owner.

with any of these genetic disorders, but they should be discussed with the breeder from whom you acquire your dog. The reputable Chow breeder is aware of the following problems and should be more than willing to discuss them with you.

Hip Dysplasia (HD)

Commonly referred to as HD, this is an orthopedic problem that affects many breeds of dog and Chow Chows are no exception. It is a malformation of the hip joints. It usually occurs bilaterally, meaning in both hips. It can occur in varying degrees from the mildest form, which is undetectable other than by x-ray, on through to extremely serious and painful cases, which may require surgery.

A simple explanation of the disease is as follows. The normal hip can best be described as a ball and socket arrangement. The upper bone of the rear leg (femur)

has a head that should fit neatly and firmly into the socket of the pelvis. A well-knit ball and socket allows the femur to rotate freely within the socket but be held firmly in place. When hip dysplasia exists, the socket is shallow, allowing the femur head to slip and slide to a greater or lesser degree. The more shallow the socket, the more it impairs movement and causes pain.

The Orthopedic Foundation for Animals (OFA) registers purebred dogs who have been cleared for hereditary orthopedic conditions like hip dysplasia and elbow dysplasia. Responsible breeders register their dogs' test results, which are provided by board-certified veterinarians. Only dogs that are graded clear of these various debilitating diseases should be bred. Likewise, the Canine Eye Registration Foundation (CERF) provides a similar service for hereditary eye diseases, like progressive retinal atrophy (PRA)

HIP DYSPLASIA

Hip dysplasia (HD) is a condition which is considered to be polygenetic. This means it is created by the interaction of several genes, making it extremely hard to predict. Although it can be detected in the individual adult dog, it is only the law of averages that reduces the occurrence when breeding individual dogs x-rayed clear of the problem.

Do You Know about Hip Dysplasia?

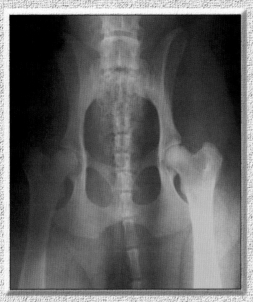

X-ray of a dog with "Good" hips.

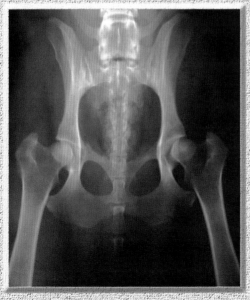

X-ray of a dog with "Moderate" dysplastic hips.

Hip dysplasia is a fairly common condition found in pure-bred dogs. When a dog has hip dysplasia, his hind leg has an incorrectly formed hip joint. By constant use of the hip joint, it becomes more and more loose, wears abnormally and may become arthritic.

Hip dysplasia can only be confirmed with an x-ray, but certain symptoms may indicate a problem. Your dog may have a hip dysplasia problem if he walks in a peculiar manner, hops instead of smoothly runs, uses his hind legs in unison (to keep the pressure off the weak joint), has trouble getting up from a prone position or always sits with both legs together on one side of his body.

As the dog matures, he may adapt well to life with a bad hip, but in a few years the arthritis develops and many dogs with hip dysplasia become crippled.

Hip dysplasia is considered an inherited disease and only can be diagnosed definitively by x-ray when the dog is two years old, although symptoms often appear earlier. Some experts claim that a special diet might help your puppy outgrow the bad hip, but the usual treatments are surgical. The removal of the pectineus muscle, the removal of the round part of the femur, reconstructing the pelvis and replacing the hip with an artificial one are all surgical interventions that are expensive, but they are usually very successful. Follow the advice of your veterinarian.

severely damage vision. A simple veterinary procedure can fully correct the condition.

Ectropion: A condition of the eyelid that causes the lid to roll out and hang down exposing the eye itself. The sagging eyelid forms a pocket that traps debris that constantly irritates the eye. This condition can also be corrected with surgery.

and cataracts. Breeders will gladly provide OFA and CERF records for the sire and dam of their litters to potential owners.

OSTEOCHONDRITIS DISSECANS (OCD)

OCD is a condition in which the cartilage lining the bone surfaces in the shoulder joint, elbow or stifle and hock joints is thickened to the point where it enlarges and cracks, allowing the bone beneath it to become inflamed and deteriorate. The degree to which it takes place causes lameness varying from an occasional limp to a chronic condition. In Chows the area most commonly affected is the elbow and is referred to as elbow dysplasia (ED).

EYE PROBLEMS

Entropion: The eyelids are turned inward so that the eye lashes constantly rub against and irritate the eyeball itself. Untreated it can

PATELLAR LUXATION

This condition, also known as slipped stifle, can be found in one or both knees of the Chow. The ligament that holds the patella, or kneecap, in place can be so weak as to slip from the groove in which it would normally fit to bind the upper and lower thigh together. It can be painful and can cause limping in some cases.

BREED STANDARD FOR THE

CHOW CHOW

The Chow Chow with the right make and shape, balance and proportion is an imposing and beautiful sight to behold. The question arises, however, what is it that tells us if a Chow Chow does in fact have "the right make and shape, balance and proportion?" Wouldn't the opinion of one fellow be as valid as the next?

Granted, your Chow Chow does not have to be a blue ribbon contender at the Westminster Kennel Club Show, but being "blue-blooded" (pure-bred) does carry some responsibilities with it. There are characteristics for which the breed is noted and which your Chow Chow should possess.

The answers to all that makes a Chow Chow an ideal specimen are found in the American Kennel Club breed standard. Breed standards are very accurate descriptions of the ideal specimen of a given breed. Standards describe the dog physically—listing all of a breed's anatomical parts and telling how those parts should look. The standard also describes the breed's temperament, how a dog should behave, and gait, how a well-made dog should move about.

This standard is the blueprint that breeders use to fashion their breeding programs. The goal, of course, is to move one step closer to that ever-elusive picture of perfection with each succeeding generation. The breed standard is also what dog show judges use to

One of breed's top producers and show winners is Ch. Starcrest Lemon Drop Kid, pictured here with Joel Marston.

see which of the dogs being shown compares most favorably to what is required.

It should be understood that what the standard describes is the perfect dog of a given breed. In nature, nothing is absolutely perfect. Thus the breeder and the judge are looking for the dog that in their opinion has "most of the best." How each individual person interprets this will always vary somewhat, but there is usually little disagreement when a dog comes along that truly has most of what the breed standard actually specifies. No dog will have it all.

Although it takes many years to fully understand the implications of a breed standard, it behooves the prospective owner of any breed to familiarize himself with the requirements therein. This will enable the person who wishes to own a dog of that breed to be able to have a good idea of what a representative specimen should look like.

THE AMERICAN KENNEL CLUB STANDARD FOR THE CHOW CHOW

GENERAL APPEARANCE
Characteristics: An ancient breed of northern Chinese origin, this all-purpose dog of China was used for hunting, herding, pulling and protection of the home. While primarily a companion today, his working origin must always be

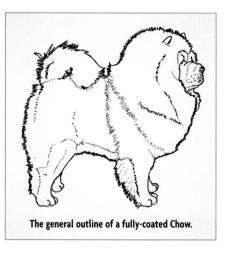

The general outline of a fully-coated Chow.

remembered when assessing true Chow type.

A powerful, sturdy, squarely built, upstanding dog of Arctic type, medium in size with strong muscular development and heavy bone. The body is compact, short coupled, broad and deep, the tail set high and carried closely to the back, the whole supported by four straight, strong, sound legs. Viewed from the side, the hind legs have little apparent angulation and the hock joint and metatarsals are directly beneath the hip joint. It is this structure which produces the characteristic short, stilted gait unique to the breed. The large head with broad, flat skull and short, broad and deep muzzle is proudly carried and accentuated by a ruff. Elegance and substance must be combined into a well balanced whole, never so massive as to outweigh his ability to be active, alert and agile. Clothed in a smooth or an offstanding rough double coat, the Chow is a masterpiece of beauty, dignity and naturalness, unique in his blue-black tongue, scowling expression and stilted gait.

SIZE, PROPORTIONS, SUBSTANCE

Size: The average height of adult specimens is 17 to 20 inches at the withers but in every case consideration of overall proportions and type should take precedence over size. **Proportions:** Square in profile and close coupled. Distance from forechest to point of buttocks equals height at the highest points of the withers. *Serious Fault:* Profile other than square. Distance from tip of elbow to ground is half the height at the withers. Floor of chest level with tips of elbows. Width viewed from the front and rear is the same and must be broad. It is these proportions that are essential to true Chow type. In judging puppies, no allowance should be made for their failure to conform to these proportions. **Substance:** Medium in size with strong muscular development and heavy bone. Equally objectionable are snipy, fine boned specimens and overdone, ponderous, cloddy specimens. In comparing specimens of different sex, due allowance must be made in favor of the bitches who may not have as much head or substance as do the males. There is an impression of femininity in bitches as compared to an impression of masculinity in dogs.

HEAD

Proudly carried, large in proportion to the size of the dog but never so exaggerated as to make

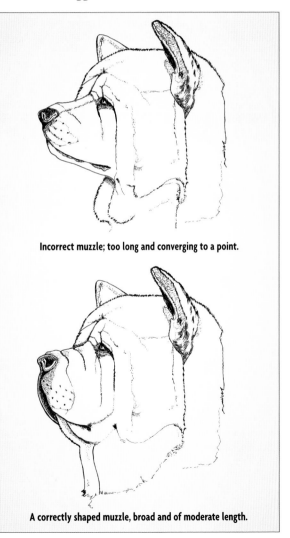

Incorrect muzzle; too long and converging to a point.

A correctly shaped muzzle, broad and of moderate length.

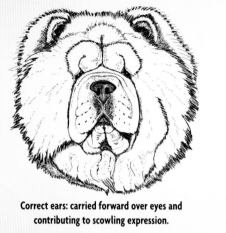

Correct ears: carried forward over eyes and contributing to scowling expression.

Incorrect ear set and carriage.

the dog seem top-heavy or to result in a low carriage. *Expression* essentially scowling, dignified, lordly, discerning, sober and snobbish, one of independence. The scowl is achieved by a marked brow with a padded button of skin just above the inner, upper corner of each eye; by sufficient play of skin to form frowning brows and a distinct furrow between the eyes beginning at the base of the muzzle and extending up the forehead; by the correct eye shape and placement and by the correct ear shape, carriage and placement. Excessive loose skin is not desirable. Wrinkles on the muzzle do not contribute to expression and are not required.

The correct Chow Chow bite should be even with a scissors bite.

Eyes: Dark brown, deep set and placed wide apart and obliquely, of moderate size, almond in shape. The correct placement and shape should create an Oriental appearance. The eye rims black with lids which neither turn in nor droop and the pupils of the eyes clearly visible. *Serious*

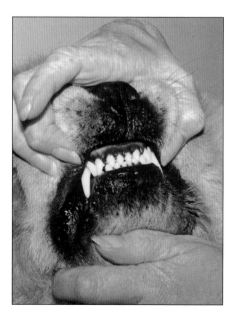

Faults: Entropion or ectropion, or pupils wholly or partially obscured by loose skin.

Ears: Small, moderately thick, triangular in shape with a slight rounding at the tip, carried stiffly erect but with a slight forward tilt. Placed wide apart with the inner corner on top of the skull. An ear which flops as the dog moves is very undesirable. *Disqualifying Fault*—Drop ear or ears. A drop ear is one which breaks at any point from its base to its tip or which is not carried stiffly erect but lies parallel to the top of the skull.

Skull: The top skull is broad and flat from side to side and front to back. Coat and loose skin cannot substitute for the correct bone structure. Viewed in profile, the

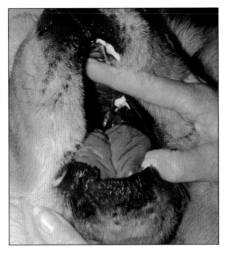

Characteristic purplish tongue; flews and roof of mouth are black.

toplines of the muzzle and skull are approximately parallel, joined by a moderate stop. The padding of the brows may make the stop appear steeper than it is. The muzzle is short in comparison to the length of the top skull but

LEFT: Smooth Chow exhibiting weak forequarters, legs turned out. MIDDLE: Rough Chow with legs that are too short. RIGHT: Correct structure of forequarters, as shown in the Smooth Chow.

never less than one-third of the head length. The muzzle is broad and well filled out under the eyes, its width and depth are equal and both dimensions should appear to be the same from its base to its tip. This square appearance is achieved by correct bone structure plus padding of the muzzle and full cushioned lips. The muzzle should never be so padded or cushioned as to make it appear other than square in shape. The upper lips completely cover the lower lips when the mouth is closed but should not be pendulous.

Nose: Large, broad and black in color with well opened nostrils. *Disqualifying Fault*—Nose spotted or distinctly other color than black, except in blue Chows which may have solid blue or slate noses.

Mouth and Tongue: Edges of the lips black, tissues of the mouth mostly black, gums preferably black. A solid black mouth is ideal. The top surface and edges of the tongue a solid blue-black, the darker the better. *Disqualifying Fault*—The top surface or edges of the tongue red or pink or with one or more spots of red or pink. Teeth strong and even with a scissors bite.

NECK, TOPLINE, BODY
Neck: Strong, full, well muscled, nicely arched and of sufficient length to carry the head proudly

MEETING THE IDEAL
The American Kennel Club defines a standard as: "A description of the ideal dog of each recognized breed, to serve as an ideal against which dogs are judged at shows." This "blueprint" is drawn up by the breed's recognized parent club, approved by a majority of its membership, and then submitted to the AKC for approval. This is a complete departure from the way standards are handled in England, where all standards and changes are controlled by The Kennel Club.

The picture that the standard draws of the dog's type, gait, temperament and structure is the guiding image used by breeders as they plan their programs.

above the topline when standing at attention. Topline straight, strong and level from the withers to the root of the tail.

Body: Short, compact, close coupled, strongly muscled, broad, deep and well let down in the flank. The body, back, coupling and croup must all be short to give the required square build. Chest broad, deep and muscular, never narrow or slab-sided. The ribs close together and well sprung, not barrel. The spring of the front ribs is somewhat narrowed at their lower ends to permit the shoulder and upper arm to fit smoothly against the chest wall. The floor of the chest is broad and deep extending down to the tips of the elbows. The point of sternum slightly in front of the shoulder points. *Serious Faults*: Labored or abdominal breathing (not to include normal panting), narrow or slab-sided chest. Loin well muscled, strong, short, broad and deep. Croup short and broad with powerful rump and thigh muscles giving a level croup. Tail set high and carried closely to the back at all times, following the line of the spine at the start.

FOREQUARTERS

Shoulders: Strong, well muscled, the tips of the shoulder blades moderately close together; the spine of the shoulder forms an angle approximately 55 degrees with the horizontal and forms an angle with the upper arm of approximately 110 degrees resulting in less reach of the forelegs. Length of upper arm never less than length of shoulder blade. Elbow joints set well back alongside the chest wall, elbows turning neither in nor out. **Forelegs:** Perfectly straight from elbow to foot with heavy bone which must be in proportion to the rest of the dog. Viewed from the front, the forelegs are parallel and widely spaced commensurate with the broad chest. **Pasterns:** Short and upright. Wrists shall not knuckle over. The dewclaws may be removed. **Feet:** Round, compact,

catlike, standing well up on the thick toe pads.

HINDQUARTERS

The rear assembly broad, powerful, and well muscled in the hips and thighs, heavy in bone with rear and front bone approximately equal. Viewed from the rear, the legs are straight, parallel and widely spaced commensurate with the broad pelvis. **Stifle Joint:** Shows little angulation, is well knit and stable, points straight forward and the bones of the joint should be clean and sharp. **Hock Joint:** Well let down and appears almost straight. The hock joint must be strong, well knit and firm, never bowing or breaking forward or to either side. The hock joint and metatarsals lie in a straight line below the hip joint. *Serious Faults*: Unsound stifle or hock joints. **Metatarsals:** Short and perpendicular to the ground. The dewclaws may be removed. **Feet:** Same as front.

LEFT: Weak hindquarters; over-angulated.
RIGHT: Correct hindquarters with minimal angulation.

Rear view of adult and pup showing correct tail set and carriage.

COAT

There are two types of coat; rough and smooth. Both are double coated. **Rough:** In the rough coat, the outer coat is abundant, dense, straight and offstanding, rather coarse in texture; the undercoat soft, thick and wooly. Puppy coat soft, thick and wooly overall. The coat forms a profuse ruff around the head and neck, framing the head. The coat and ruff generally longer in dogs than in bitches. Tail well feathered. The coat length varies markedly on different Chows and thickness, texture and condition should be given greater emphasis than length. Obvious trimming or shaping is undesirable. Trimming of the whiskers, feet and metatarsals optional. **Smooth:** The smooth coated Chow is judged by the same standard as the rough coated Chow except that references to the quantity and distribution of the outer coat are not applicable to the smooth coated Chow, which has a hard, dense, smooth outer coat with a definite undercoat. There should be no obvious ruff or feathering on the legs or tail.

COLOR

Clear colored, solid or solid with lighter shadings in the ruff, tail and featherings. There are five colors in the Chow: red (light golden to deep mahogany), black, blue, cinnamon (light fawn to deep cinnamon) and cream. Acceptable colors to be judged on an equal basis.

GAIT

Proper movement is the crucial test of proper conformation and soundness. It must be sound, straight moving, agile, brief, quick and powerful, never lumbering. The rear gait short and stilted because of the straighter rear assembly. It is from the side that the unique stilted action is most easily assessed. The rear leg moves up and forward from the hip in a straight, stilted pendulum-like line with a slight bounce in the rump, the legs extend neither far forward nor far backward. The hind foot has a strong thrust which transfers power to the body in an almost straight line due to the minimal rear leg angulation. To transmit this power efficiently to the front assembly, the coupling must be short and there should be no roll through the midsection. Viewed from the rear, the line of bone from hip joint to pad remains straight as the dog moves. As the speed increases the hind legs incline slightly inward. The stifle joints must point in the line of travel, not outward resulting in a bowlegged appearance nor hitching in under the dog. Viewed from the front, the line of bone from shoulder joint to pad remains straight as the dog moves. As the speed increases, the forelegs do not move in exact parallel planes, rather, incline slightly inward. The front legs must not swing out in semicircles nor mince or show any evidence of hackney action. The front and rear assemblies must be in dynamic equilibrium. Somewhat lacking in speed, the Chow has excellent endurance because the sound, straight rear leg provides direct, usable power efficiently.

TEMPERAMENT
Keen intelligence, an independent spirit and innate dignity give the Chow an aura of aloofness. It is a Chow's nature to be reserved and discerning with strangers. Displays of aggression or timidity are unacceptable. Because of its deep set eyes the Chow has limited peripheral vision and is best approached within the scope of that vision.

SUMMARY
Faults shall be penalized in proportion to their deviation from the standard. In judging the Chow,

The short, stilted gait of the Chow.

the overall picture is of primary consideration. Exaggeration of any characteristic at the expense of balance or soundness shall be severely penalized.

Type should include general appearance, temperament, the harmony of all parts, and soundness especially as seen when the dog is in motion. There should be proper emphasis on movement which is the final test of the Chow's conformation, balance and soundness.

DISQUALIFICATIONS
Drop ear or ears. A drop ear is one which breaks at any point from its base to its tip or which is not carried stiffly erect but lies parallel to the top of the skull.

Nose spotted or distinctly other color than black, except in blue Chows which may have solid blue or slate noses.

The top surface or edges of the tongue red or pink or with one or more spots of red or pink.

Approved November 11, 1986
Reformatted August 21, 1990

CHOW CHOW

WHERE TO BUY YOUR CHOW

Barring accidents, your Chow will live with you for many years. It is not at all surprising to see Chows live to be 10, 12 and often 14 years of age. It is extremely important, therefore, that the Chow puppy you purchase comes from a source where physical and mental soundness are primary considerations in the breeding program.

Achieving this goal is usually the result of careful breeding over a period of many years. Selective breeding is aimed at maintaining the virtues of the breed and eliminating genetic weaknesses. Because this selective breeding is time-consuming and costly, good breeders protect their investment by providing the best prenatal care for their breeding females and nutrition for the growing puppies. There is no substitute for the amount of dedication and care good breeders give their dogs.

All this is not to imply your Chow puppy must come from a large kennel. On the contrary, many good puppies are produced by small hobby breeders in their homes. These names may well be included in recommendations from the American Kennel Club and from local Chow Chow clubs. These individuals offer the same investment of time, study and knowledge as the larger kennel and often the puppies receive better hands-on socialization, especially important with the Chow Chow breed.

Do not be surprised if a concerned breeder asks many questions about you and the environment in which your Chow will be raised. A responsible breeder will want to know if you have a fenced yard, if there are young children in the family and if someone will be home with the young puppy during the course of an average day. Good breeders are

---

THE FIRST FAMILY MEETING

Your puppy's first day at home should be quiet and uneventful. Despite his wagging tail, he is still wondering where his mom and siblings are! Let him make friends with other members of the family on his own terms; don't overwhelm him. You have a lifetime ahead to get to know each other.

MALE OR FEMALE?

Males of most dog breeds tend to be larger than their female counterparts and take longer to mature. Males also can be more dominant and territorial, especially if they are intact. Neutering before one year of age can help minimize those tendencies. Females of most breeds are often less rambunctious and easier to handle. However, individual personalities vary, so the differences are often due more to temperament than to the sex of the animal.

just as concerned with the quality of the homes to which their dogs are going as you, the buyer, are in obtaining a sound and healthy dog.

PURCHASING THE CHOW PUPPY

Most likely you are seeking a Chow for a companion dog and not necessarily for a show dog. If dog shows hold an interest, do let the breeder you are considering know this at the outset. Breeders are normally most anxious to find

Decide whether you want a pet-quality or show-quality Chow puppy before you start shopping.

HOMEBOUND TODDLERS

Breeders rarely release puppies until they are eight to ten weeks of age. This is an acceptable age for most breeds of dog, excepting toy breeds, which are not released until around 12 weeks, given their petite sizes. If a breeder has a puppy that is 12 weeks or more, it is likely well socialized and house-trained. Be sure that it is otherwise healthy before deciding to take it home.

show homes for those extra-special puppies that come along every once in a while.

But if it is strictly a pet you are seeking, that does not mean you are looking for a second-rate model. A pet-quality Chow is not like a second-hand car or a "slightly irregular" suit jacket. Your pet must be as sound,

healthy and temperamentally fit as any top show dog.

Pet owners do not want a Chow who isn't sound of both body and mind, who is not trust-worthy and reliable around children and strangers. Nor do they want one that doesn't look like a Chow. You are not buying a reject, you want an impressive dog with the leonine expression that typi-fies the breed—a dog that has sound hips, good eyes and a love-able personality.

Inquire about inoculations and when the puppy was last dosed for worms. Check the ears for any signs of mites or irritation. Are the eyes clear and free of any debris? The puppy coat is softer and fluffier than the adult coat and it should feel silky and clean to the touch. The Chow comes in a large range of colors, and if dog shows are not in your dog's future, the color that appeals most to you is the one you should choose.

Never settle for anything less than a happy, healthy outgoing puppy. A Chow puppy should love the world and everyone in it. As playful as the puppy might be, it should not object to being held. Chow puppies that panic and struggle to be released have proba-bly not had proper socialization or might have inherited anti-social behavior.

In total the Chow's head is massive and its expression is

scowling and aloof. Perhaps less scowling and aloof in puppyhood but still giving you an indication of what is to come.

Check the mouth to make sure that the bite is fairly even. Maturity can correct errors in dentition that are present at puppyhood, but never select a puppy that has any deformities of the mouth or jaw.

Pay attention to the way your selection moves. The Chow in puppyhood (particularly at eight weeks) is a miniaturized replica of what it looks like at maturity. Short and stylish-looking with sound, deliberate movement, which may appear a bit wooden in puppyhood. There should be no inclination to stumble or limp. Do realize, though, that the chubby little boy puppies might be a bit more awkward than their slightly more svelte sisters, so do make allowances.

A COMMITTED NEW OWNER

By now you should understand what makes the Chow a most unique and special dog, one that may fit nicely into your family and lifestyle. If you have researched breeders, you should be able to recognize a knowledge-able and responsible Chow breeder who cares not only about his pups but also about what kind of owner you will be. If you have completed the final step in your new journey, you have found a

A SOLID LITTLE PUPPY
Your puppy should have a well-fed appearance but not a distended abdomen, which may indicate worms or incorrect feeding, or both. The body should be firm, with a solid feel. The skin of the abdomen should be pale pink and clean, without signs of scratching or rash. Check the hind legs to make certain that dewclaws were removed, if any were present at birth.

litter, or possibly two, of quality Chow pups.

A visit with the puppies and their breeder should be an education in itself. Breed research, breeder selection and puppy visitation are very important aspects of finding the puppy of your dreams. Beyond that, these things also lay the foundation for a

SELECTING FROM THE LITTER

Before you visit a litter of puppies, promise yourself that you won't fall for the first pretty face you see! Decide on your goals for your puppy—show prospect, therapy dog, obedience competitor, family companion—and then look for a puppy who displays the appropriate qualities. In most litters, there is an Alpha pup (the bossy puppy), and occasionally a shy fellow who is less confident, with the rest of the litter falling somewhere in the middle. "Middle-of-the-roaders" are safe bets for most families and novice competitors.

successful future with your pup. Puppy personalities within each litter vary, from the shy and easy-going puppy to the one who is dominant and assertive, with most pups falling somewhere in between. By spending time with the puppies you will be able to recognize certain behaviors and what these behaviors indicate about each pup's temperament. Which type of pup will complement your family dynamics is best determined by observing the

puppies in action within their "pack." Your breeder's expertise and recommendations are also valuable. Although you may fall in love with a bold and brassy male, the breeder may suggest that another pup would be best for you. The breeder's experience in rearing Chow pups and matching their temperaments with appropriate humans offers the best assurance that your pup will meet your needs and expectations. The type of puppy that you select is just as important as your decision that the Chow is the breed for you.

The decision to live with a Chow is a serious commitment and not one to be taken lightly. This puppy is a living sentient being that will be dependent on you for basic survival for his entire life. Beyond the basics of survival—food, water, shelter and protection—he needs much, much more. The new pup needs love, nurturing and a proper canine education to mold him into a responsible, well-behaved canine citizen. Your Chow's health and good manners will need consistent monitoring and regular "tune-ups," so your job as a responsible dog owner will be ongoing throughout every stage of his life. If you are not prepared to accept these responsibilities and commit to them for the next decade, likely longer, then you are not prepared to own a dog of any breed.

Although the responsibilities of owning a dog may at times tax your patience, the joy of living with your Chow far outweighs the workload, and a well-mannered adult dog is worth your time and effort. Before your very eyes, your new charge will grow up to be your most loyal friend, devoted to you unconditionally.

YOUR CHOW SHOPPING LIST

Just as expectant parents prepare a nursery for their baby, so should you ready your home for the arrival of your Chow pup. If you have the necessary puppy supplies purchased and in place before he comes home, it will ease the puppy's transition from the warmth and familiarity of his mom and littermates to the brand-new environment of his new home and human family. You will be too busy to stock up and prepare your house after your pup comes home, that's for sure! Imagine how a pup must feel upon being transported to a strange new place. It's up to you to comfort him and to let your little pup know that he is going to be happy with you.

Lavish love and affection on your new Chow puppy. Soon he will blossom into a loving, happy pet.

TEMPERAMENT ABOVE ALL ELSE

When selecting a Chow pet, a puppy's disposition is his most important quality. It is, after all, what makes a puppy lovable and "livable." If the puppy's parents or grandparents are known to be snappy or aggressive, the puppy is likely to inherit those tendencies. That can lead to serious problems, such as the dog's becoming a biter, which can lead to eventual abandonment.

FOOD AND WATER BOWLS

Your puppy will need separate bowls for his food and water. Stainless steel pans are generally preferred over plastic bowls since they sterilize better and pups are less inclined to chew on the

CRATE EXPECTATIONS

To make the crate more inviting to your puppy, you can offer his first meal or two inside the crate, always keeping the crate door open so that he does not feel confined. Keep a favorite toy or two in the crate for him to play with while inside. You can also cover the crate at night with a lightweight sheet to make it more den-like and remove the stimuli of household activity. Never put him into his crate as punishment or as you are scolding him, since he will then associate his crate with negative situations and avoid going there.

house," a cozy place to sleep, take a break or seek comfort with a favorite toy; a travel aid to house your dog when on the road, at motels or at the vet's office; a training aid to help teach your puppy proper toileting habits; a place of solitude when non-dog people happen to drop by and don't want a lively puppy—or even a well-behaved adult dog—saying hello or begging for attention.

Crates come in several types, although the wire crate and the fiberglass airline-type crate are the most popular. Both are safe and your puppy will adjust to either one, so the choice is up to you. The wire crates offer better visibility for the pup as well as better ventilation. Many of the wire crates easily collapse into suitcase-size carriers. The fiberglass

metal. Heavy-duty ceramic bowls are popular, but consider how often you will have to pick up those heavy bowls! Buy adult-sized pans, as your puppy will grow into them before you know it.

Be sure the crate you buy will be large enough for the fully grown Chow.

The Dog Crate

If you think that crates are tools of punishment and confinement for when a dog has misbehaved, think again. Most breeders and almost all trainers recommend a crate as the preferred house-training aid as well as for all-around puppy training and safety. Because dogs are natural den creatures that prefer cave-like environments, the benefits of crate use are many. The crate provides the puppy with his very own "safe

crates, similar to those used by the airlines for animal transport, are sturdier and more den-like. However, the fiberglass crates do not collapse and are less ventilated than a wire crate, which can be problematic in hot weather. Some of the newer crates are made of heavy plastic mesh; they are very lightweight and fold up into slim-line suitcases. However, a mesh crate might not be suitable for a pup with manic chewing habits.

Don't bother with a puppy-sized crate. Although your Chow will be a wee fellow when you bring him home, he will grow up in the blink of an eye and your puppy crate will be useless. Purchase a crate that will accommodate an adult Chow. He will stand about 20 inches when full grown, so a medium- to large-sized crate will fit him nicely.

BEDDING AND CRATE PADS

Your puppy will enjoy some type of soft bedding in his "room" (the crate), something he can snuggle into to feel cozy and secure. Old towels or blankets are good choices for a young pup, since he may (and probably will) have a toileting accident or two in the crate or decide to chew on the bedding material. Once he is fully trained and out of the early chewing stage, you can replace the puppy bedding with a permanent crate pad if you prefer. Crate pads

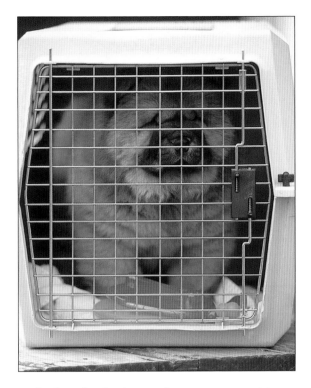

and other dog beds run the gamut from inexpensive to high-end doggie-designer styles, but don't splurge on the good stuff until you are sure that your puppy is reliable and won't tear it up or make a mess on it.

One of the advantages offered by a sturdy crate is that it provides a safe refuge during travel.

PUPPY TOYS

Just as infants and older children require objects to stimulate their minds and bodies, puppies need toys to entertain their curious brains, wiggly paws and achy teeth. A fun array of safe doggie toys will help satisfy your puppy's chewing instincts and distract him from gnawing on the leg of your antique chair or your new leather sofa. Most puppy toys are cute and look as if they would be a lot of fun, but not all are necessarily safe or good for your puppy, so use caution when you go puppy-toy shopping.

Although Chows are not known to be voracious chewers like many other dogs, they still love to chew. The best "chewci-fiers" are nylon and hard rubber bones which are safe to gnaw on and come in sizes appropriate for all age groups and breeds. Be especially careful of natural bones, which can splinter or develop dangerous sharp edges; pups can easily swallow or choke on those bone splinters. Veterinar-ians often tell of surgical night-mares involving bits of splintered bone, because in addition to the danger of choking, the sharp pieces can damage the intestinal tract.

Similarly, rawhide chews, while a favorite of most dogs and

An enormous variety of dog toys is offered at pet shops, but not all are equally safe.

> ### TOYS 'R SAFE
> The vast array of tantalizing puppy toys is staggering. Stroll through any pet shop or pet-supply outlet and you will see that the choices can be overwhelming. However, not all dog toys are safe or sensible. Most very young puppies enjoy soft woolly toys that they can snuggle with and carry around. (You know they have outgrown them when they shred them up!) Avoid toys that have buttons, tabs or other enhancements that can be chewed off and swallowed. Soft toys that squeak are fun, but make sure your puppy does not disembowel the toy and remove (and swallow) the squeaker. Toys that rattle or make noise can excite a puppy, but they present the same danger as the squeaky kind and so require supervision. Hard rubber toys that bounce can also entertain a pup, but make sure that the toy is too big for your pup to swallow.

puppies, can be equally danger-ous. Pieces of rawhide are easily swallowed after they get all gummy from chewing, and dogs have been known to choke on large pieces of ingested rawhide. Rawhide chews should be offered only when you can supervise the puppy.

Soft woolly toys are special puppy favorites. They come in a wide variety of cute shapes and sizes; some look like little stuffed animals. Puppies love to shake them up and toss them

about, or simply carry them around. Be careful of fuzzy toys that have button eyes or noses that your pup could chew off and swallow, and make sure that he does not disembowel a squeaky toy to remove the squeaker! Braided rope toys are similar in that they are fun to chew and toss around, but they shred easily and the strings are easy to swallow. The strings are not digestible and, if the puppy doesn't pass them in his stool, he could end up at the vet's office. As with rawhides, your puppy should be closely monitored with rope toys.

If you believe that your pup has ingested one of these forbidden objects, check his stools for the next couple of days to see if he passes them when he defecates. At the same time, also watch for signs of intestinal distress. A call to your veterinarian might be in order to get his advice and be on the safe side.

An all-time favorite toy for puppies (young and old!) is the empty gallon milk jug. Hard plastic juice containers—46 ounces or more—are also excellent. Such containers make lots of noise when they are batted about, and puppies go crazy with delight as they play with them. However, they don't often last very long, so be sure to remove and replace them when they get chewed up on the ends.

A word of caution about homemade toys: be careful with your choices of non-traditional play objects. Never use old shoes or socks, since a puppy cannot distinguish between the old ones on which he's allowed to chew and the new ones in your closet that are strictly off limits. That principle applies to anything that resembles something that you don't want your puppy to chew up.

Dogs of all ages, like to chew, but you should exercise care about what they're allowed to chew on.

COLLARS
A lightweight nylon collar is the best choice for a very young pup. Quick-clip collars are easy to put on and remove, and they can be adjusted as the puppy grows. Introduce him to his collar as

The first collar and lead you buy for your Chow puppy should be very light and not overpowering.

soon as he comes home to get him accustomed to wearing it. He'll get used to it quickly and won't mind a bit. Make sure that it is snug enough that it won't slip off, yet loose enough to be comfortable for the pup. You should be able to slip two fingers between the collar and his neck. Check the collar often, as puppies grow in spurts, and his collar can become too tight almost overnight. Choke collars are for training purposes only and should never be used on a puppy under four or five months old.

LEASHES

A 6-foot nylon lead is an excellent choice for a young puppy. It is lightweight and not as tempting to chew as a leather lead. You can switch to a 6-foot leather lead after your pup has grown and is used to walking politely on a lead. For initial puppy walks and house-training purposes, you

should invest in a shorter lead so that you have more control over the puppy. At first, you don't want him wandering too far away from you, and when taking him out for toileting you will want to keep him in the specific area chosen for his potty spot.

Once the puppy is heel trained with a traditional leash, you can consider purchasing a retractable lead. This type of lead is excellent for walking adult dogs that are already leash-wise. The retractable lead allows the dog to roam farther away from you and explore a wider area when out walking, and also retracts when you need to keep him close to you.

HOME SAFETY FOR YOUR PUPPY

The importance of puppy-proofing cannot be overstated. In addition to making your house comfortable for your Chow's arrival, you also must make sure that your house is safe for your puppy before you bring him home. There are countless hazards in the owner's personal living environment that a pup can sniff, chew, swallow or destroy. Many are obvious; others are not. Do a thorough advance house check to remove or rearrange those things that could hurt your puppy, keeping any potentially dangerous items out of areas to which he will have access.

Electrical cords are especially dangerous, since puppies view them as irresistible chew toys. Unplug and remove all exposed cords or fasten them beneath a baseboard where the puppy cannot reach them. Veterinarians and firefighters can tell you horror stories about electrical burns and house fires that resulted from puppy-chewed electrical cords. Consider this a most serious precaution for your puppy and the rest of your family.

KEEP OUT OF REACH

Most dogs don't browse around your medicine cabinet, but accidents do happen! The drug acetaminophen, the active ingredient in Tylenol®, can be deadly to dogs and cats if ingested in large quantities. Acetaminophen toxicity, caused by the dog's swallowing 15 to 20 tablets, can be manifested in abdominal pains within a day or two of ingestion, as well as liver damage. If you suspect your dog has swiped a bottle of Tylenol®, get the dog to the vet immediately so that the vet can induce vomiting and cleanse the dog's stomach.

Scout your home for tiny objects that might be seen at a pup's eye level. Keep medication bottles and cleaning supplies well out of reach, and do the same with waste baskets and other trash containers. It goes without saying that you should not use rodent poison or other toxic chemicals in any puppy area and that you must keep such containers safely locked up. You will be amazed at how many places a curious puppy can discover!

Once your house has cleared inspection, check your yard. A sturdy fence, well embedded into the ground, will give your dog a safe place to play and potty. Although Chows are not known to be climbers or fence jumpers, they

Wire crates or pens serve many useful purposes. They are lightweight and easy to carry, as they fold down and can be quickly reassembled.

A doghouse in the yard will provide the Chow with a shady place to rest.

COLLARING OUR CANINES

The standard flat collar with a buckle or a snap, in leather, nylon or cotton, is widely regarded as the everyday all-purpose collar. If the collar fits correctly, you should be able to fit two fingers between the collar and the dog's neck. The martingale, greyhound or limited-slip collar is preferred by many dog owners and trainers. It is

Leather Buckle Collars

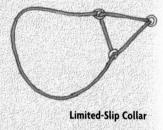

Limited-Slip Collar

fixed with an extra loop that tightens when pressure is applied to the leash. The martingale collar gets tighter but does not "choke" the dog. The limited-slip collar should only be used for walking and training, not for free play or interaction with another dog. These types of collar should never be left on the dog, as the extra loop can lead to accidents.

Choke collars, usually made of stainless steel, are made for training purposes, though are not recommended for small dogs or heavily coated breeds. The chains can injure small dogs or damage long/abundant coats. Thin nylon choke leads are commonly used on show dogs while in the ring, though they are not practical for everyday use.

The harness, with two or three straps that attach over the dog's shoulders and around his torso, is a humane and safe alternative to the conventional collar. By and large, a well-made harness is virtually escape-proof. Harnesses are available in nylon and mesh and can be outfitted on most dogs, ranging from chest girths of 10 to 30 inches.

Snap Bolt Choke Collar

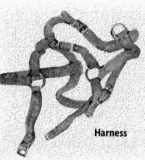

Harness

Nylon Collar

Quick-Click Closure

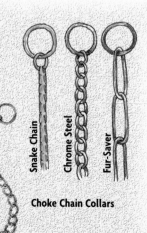

Snake Chain   Chrome Steel   Fur-Saver

Choke Chain Collars

A head collar, composed of a nylon strap that goes around the dog's muzzle and a second strap that wraps around his neck, offers the owner better control over his dog. This device is recommended for problem-solving with dogs (including jumping up, pulling and aggressive behaviors), but must be used with care.

A training halter, including a flat collar and two straps, made of nylon and webbing, is designed for walking. There are several on the market; some are more difficult to put on the dog than others. The halter harness, with two small slip rings at each end, is recommended for ease of use.

Leash Life

Dogs love leashes! Believe it or not, most dogs dance for joy every time their owners pick up their leashes. The leash means that the dog is going for a walk—and there are few things more exciting than that! Here are some of the kinds of leashes that are commercially available.

Nylon Leash

Leather Leash

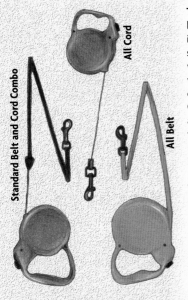

All Cord

Standard Belt and Cord Combo

All Belt

Retractable Leashes

Traditional Leash: Made of cotton, nylon or leather, these leashes are usually about 6 feet in length. A quality-made leather leash is softer on the hands than a nylon one. Durable woven cotton is a popular option. Lengths can vary up to about 48 feet, designed for different uses.

Chain Leash: Usually a metal chain leash with a plastic handle. This is not the best choice for most breeds, as it is heavier than other leashes and difficult to manage.

Retractable Leash: A long nylon cord is housed in a plastic device for extending and retracting. This leash, is ideal for taking trained dogs for long walks in open areas, although it is not recommended for large, powerful breeds. Different lengths and sizes are available, so check that you purchase one appropriate for your dog's weight.

Elastic Leash: A nylon leash with an elastic extension. This is useful for well-trained dogs, especially in conjunction with a head halter.

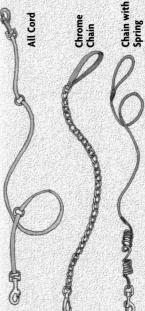

All Cord

Chrome Chain

Chain with Spring

Avoid leashes that are completely elastic, as they afford minimal control to the handler.

Adjustable Leash: This has two snaps, one on each end, and several metal rings. It is handy if you need to tether your dog temporarily, but is never to be used with a choke collar.

Tab Leash: A short leash (4 to 6 inches long) that attaches to your dog's collar. This device serves like a handle, in case you have to grab your dog while he's exercising off lead. It's ideal for "half-trained" dogs or dogs that listen only half the time.

Slip Leash: Essentially a leash with a collar built in, similar to what a dog-show handler uses to show a dog. This British-style collar has a ring on the end so that you can form a slip collar. Useful if you have to catch your own runaway dog or a stray.

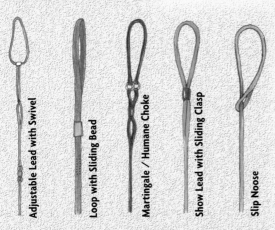

Adjustable Lead with Swivel

Loop with Sliding Bead

Martingale / Humane Choke

Show Lead with Sliding Clasp

Slip Noose

A Variety of Collar-and-Leash-in-One Products

are still athletic dogs, so a 5- to 6-foot-high fence should be adequate to contain an agile youngster or adult. Check the fence periodically for necessary repairs. If there is a weak link or space to squeeze through, you can be sure a determined Chow will discover it.

The garage and shed can be hazardous places for a pup, as things like fertilizers, chemicals and tools are usually kept there. It's best to keep these areas off limits to the pup. Antifreeze is especially dangerous to dogs, as they find the taste appealing and it takes only a few licks from the

Inoculations are necessary to keep your Chow puppy safe from debilitating and possibly fatal diseases.

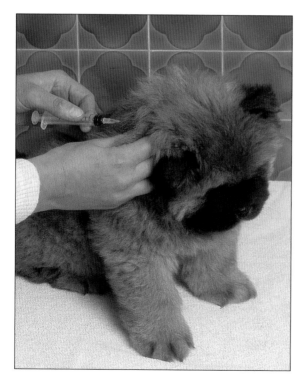

> **ASK THE VET**
> Help your vet help you to become a well-informed dog owner. Don't be shy about becoming involved in your puppy's veterinary care by asking questions and gaining as much knowledge as you can. For starters, ask what shots your puppy is getting and what diseases they prevent, and discuss with your vet the safest way to vaccinate. Find out what is involved in your dog's annual wellness visits. If you plan to spay or neuter, discuss the best age at which to have this done. Start out on the right "paw" with your puppy's vet and develop good communication with him, as he will care for your dog's health throughout the dog's entire life.

driveway to kill a dog, puppy or adult, Chow or otherwise.

VISITING THE VETERINARIAN
A good veterinarian is your Chow puppy's best health insurance policy. If you do not already have a vet, ask friends and experienced dog people in your area for recommendations so that you can select a vet before you bring your Chow puppy home. Also arrange for your puppy's first veterinary examination beforehand, since many vets have two- and three-week waiting periods, and your puppy should visit the vet within a day or so of coming home.

It's important to make sure your puppy's first visit to the vet

A Dog-Safe Home

The dog-safety police are taking you and your new puppy on a house tour. Let's go room by room and see how safe your own home is for your new pup. The following items are doggie dangers, so either they must be removed or the dog should be monitored or not have access to these areas.

Living Room

- house plants (some varieties are poisonous)
- fireplace or wood-burning stove
- paint on the walls (lead-based paint is toxic)
- lead drapery weights (toxic lead)
- lamps and electrical cords
- carpet cleaners or deodorizers

Outdoor

- swimming pool
- pesticides
- toxic plants
- lawn fertilizers

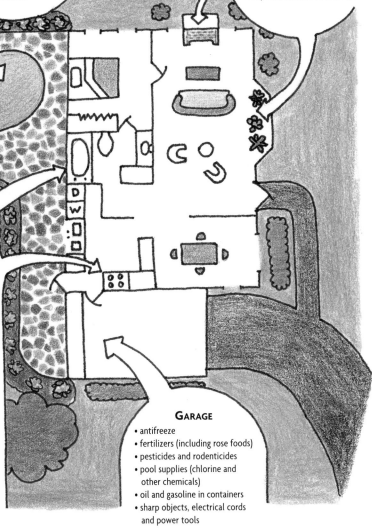

Bathroom

- blue water in the toilet bowl
- medicine cabinet (filled with potentially deadly bottles)
- soap bars, bleach, drain cleaners, etc.
- tampons

Kitchen

- household cleaners in the kitchen cabinets
- glass jars and canisters
- sharp objects (like kitchen knives, scissors and forks)
- garbage can (with remnants of good-smelling things like onions, potato skins, apple or pear cores, peach pits, coffee beans, etc.)

Garage

- antifreeze
- fertilizers (including rose foods)
- pesticides and rodenticides
- pool supplies (chlorine and other chemicals)
- oil and gasoline in containers
- sharp objects, electrical cords and power tools

Many Chows are naturally one-person dogs. Do not spoil your Chow's temperament by not sharing your bundle of Chinese love with your family and friends.

MEETING THE FAMILY

Your Chow's homecoming is an exciting time for all members of the family, and it's only natural that everyone will be eager to meet him, pet him and play with him. However, for the puppy's sake, it's best to make these initial family meetings as uneventful as possible so that the pup is not overwhelmed with too much too soon. Remember, he has just left his dam and his littermates and is away from the breeder's home for the first time. Despite his fuzzy wagging tail, he is still apprehensive and wondering where he is and who all these strange humans are. It's best to let him explore on his own and meet the family members as he feels comfortable. Let him investigate

is a pleasant and positive one. The vet should take great care to befriend the pup and handle him gently to make their first meeting a positive experience. The vet will give the pup a thorough physical examination and set up a schedule for vaccinations and other necessary wellness visits. Be sure to show your vet any health and inoculation records, which you should have received from your breeder. Your vet is a great source of canine health information, so be sure to ask questions and take notes. Creating a health journal for your puppy will make a handy reference for his wellness and any future health problems that may arise.

THE CRITICAL SOCIALIZATION PERIOD

Canine research has shown that a puppy's 8th through 16th week is the most critical learning period of his life. This is when the puppy "learns to learn," a time when he needs positive experiences to build confidence and stability. Puppies who are not exposed to different people and situations outside the home during this period can grow up to be fearful and sometimes aggressive. This is also the best time for puppy lessons, since he has not yet acquired any bad habits that could undermine his ability to learn.

all the new smells, sights and sounds at his own pace. Children should be especially careful to not get overly excited, use loud voices or hug the pup too tightly. Be calm, gentle and affectionate, and be ready to comfort him if he appears frightened or uneasy.

Be sure to show your puppy his new crate during this first day home. Toss a treat or two inside the crate; if he associates the crate with food, he will associate the crate with good things. If he is comfortable with the crate, you can offer him his first meal inside it. Leave the door ajar so he can wander in and out as he chooses.

FIRST NIGHT IN HIS NEW HOME

So much has happened in your Chow puppy's first day away from the breeder. He's had his first car ride to his new home. He's met his new human family and perhaps the other family pets. He has explored his new house and yard, at least those places where he is to be allowed during his first weeks at home. He may have visited his new veterinarian. He has eaten his first meal or two away from his dam and littermates. Surely that's enough to tire out an eight-week-old Chow pup...or so you hope!

HOUSE-TRAINING SIGNALS

Watch your puppy for signs that he has to relieve himself (sniffing, circling and squatting), and waste no time in whisking him outside to do his business. Once the puppy is older, you should attach his leash and head for the door. Puppies will always "go" immediately after they wake up, within minutes after eating and after brief periods of play, but young puppies should also be taken out regularly at times other than these, just in case! If necessary, set a timer to remind you to take him out.

It's bedtime. During the day, the pup investigated his crate, which is his new den and sleeping space, so it is not entirely strange to him. Line the crate with a soft towel or blanket that he can snuggle into and gently place him into the crate for the night. Some breeders send home a piece of

Like all other puppies, Chow puppies will chew on anything. Be sure to offer your puppy only safe toys, and make certain that your home and yard are puppy-proofed.

bedding from where the pup slept with his littermates, and those familiar scents are a great comfort for the puppy on his first night without his siblings.

Every Chow puppy must be allowed to interact with other dogs and with people at an early age so that he'll have a reliable temperament as an adult.

He will probably whine or cry. The puppy is objecting to the confinement and the fact that he is alone for the first time. This can be a stressful time for you as well as for the pup. It's important that you remain strong and don't let the puppy out of his crate to comfort him. He will fall asleep eventually. If you release him, the puppy will learn that crying means "out" and will continue that habit. You are laying the groundwork for future habits.

Some breeders find that soft music can soothe a crying pup and help him get to sleep.

SOCIALIZING YOUR PUPPY
The next 20 weeks of your Chow puppy's life are the most important of his entire lifetime. A properly socialized puppy will grow up to be a confident and stable adult who will be a pleasure to live with and a welcome addition to the neighborhood.

The importance of socialization cannot be overemphasized. Research on canine behavior has proven that puppies who are not exposed to new sights, sounds, people and animals during their first 20 weeks of life will grow up to be timid and fearful, even aggressive, and unable to flourish outside of their home environment.

Socializing your puppy is not difficult and, in fact, will be a fun time for you both. Lead training goes hand in hand with socialization, so your puppy will be learning how to walk on a lead at the same time that he's meeting the neighborhood. Because the Chow is such a fascinating breed, your puppy will enjoy being "the new kid on the block." Take him for short walks, to the park and to other dog-friendly places where he will encounter new people, especially children. Puppies automatically recognize children as "little people" and are drawn to play

will want to pet him. All of these encounters will help to mold him into a confident adult dog. Likewise, you will soon feel like a confident, responsible dog owner, rightly proud of your handsome Chow.

Be especially careful of your puppy's encounters and experiences during the eight-to-ten-week-old period, which is also called the "fear period." This is a serious imprinting period, and all contact during this time should be gentle and positive. A frightening or negative event could leave a permanent impression that could affect his future behavior if a similar situation arises.

Also make sure that your puppy has received his first and second rounds of vaccinations before you expose him to other dogs or bring him to places that

The yard should be securely fenced, with the fence examined regularly to ensure that it is in good repair.

with them. Just make sure that you supervise these meetings and that the children do not get too rough or encourage him to play too hard. An overzealous pup can often nip too hard, frightening the child and in turn making the puppy overly excited. A bad experience in puppyhood can impact a dog for life, so a pup that has a negative experience with a child may grow up to be shy or even aggressive around children.

Take your puppy along on your daily errands. Puppies are natural "people magnets," and most people who see your pup

MEET AND MINGLE

Puppies need to meet people and see the world if they are to grow up confident and unafraid. Take your puppy with you on everyday outings and errands. On-lead walks around the neighborhood and to the park offer the pup good exposure to the goings-on of his new human world. Avoid areas frequented by other dogs until your puppy has had his full round of puppy shots; ask your vet when your pup will be properly protected. Arrange for your puppy to meet new people of all ages every week.

other dogs may frequent. Avoid dog parks and other strange-dog areas until your vet assures you that your puppy is fully immunized and resistant to the diseases that can be passed between canines. Discuss socialization with your breeder, as some breeders recommend socializing the puppy even before he has received all of his inoculations, depending on how outgoing the puppy may be.

THE FAMILY FELINE

A resident cat has feline squatter's rights. The cat will treat the newcomer (your puppy) as she sees fit, regardless of what you do or say. So it's best to let the two of them work things out on their own terms. Cats have a height advantage and will generally leap to higher ground to avoid direct contact with a rambunctious pup. Some will hiss and boldly swat at a pup who passes by or tries to reach the cat. Keep the puppy under control in the presence of the cat and they will eventually become accustomed to each other.

Here's a hint: move the cat's litter box where the puppy can't get into it! It's best to do so well before the pup comes home so the cat is used to the new location.

LEADER OF THE PUPPY'S PACK

Like other canines, your puppy needs an authority figure, someone he can look up to and regard as the leader of his "pack." His first pack leader was his dam, who taught him to be polite and not chew too hard on her ears or nip at her muzzle. He learned those same lessons from his littermates. If he played too rough, they cried in pain and stopped the game, which sent an important message to the rowdy puppy.

As puppies play together, they are also struggling to determine who will be the boss. Being pack animals, dogs need someone to be in charge. If a litter of puppies remained together beyond puppyhood, one of the pups would emerge as the strongest one, the one who calls the shots.

Once your puppy leaves the pack, he will look intuitively for a new leader. If he does not recognize you as that leader, he will try to assume that position for himself. Of course, it is hard to imagine your adorable Chow puppy trying to be in charge when he is so small and seemingly helpless. You must remember that these are natural canine instincts. Do not cave in and allow your pup to get the upper "paw"!

Just as socialization is so important during these first 20 weeks, so too is your puppy's early education. He was born without any bad habits. He does not know what is good or bad behavior. If he does things like nipping and digging, it's because he is having fun and doesn't know that humans consider these things as "bad." It's your job to teach him proper puppy manners, and this is the best time to accomplish that…before he has developed bad habits, since it is much more difficult to "unlearn" or correct unacceptable learned behavior than to teach good behavior from the start.

Make sure that all members of the family understand the importance of being consistent when training their new puppy. If you tell the puppy to stay off the sofa and your daughter allows him to cuddle on the couch to watch her favorite television show, your pup will be confused about what he is and is not allowed to do. Have a family conference before your pup comes home so that everyone understands the basic principles of puppy training and the rules you have set forth for the pup, and agrees to follow them.

The old adage that "an ounce of prevention is worth a pound of

cure" is especially true when it comes to puppies. It is much easier to prevent inappropriate behavior than it is to change it. It's also easier and less stressful for the pup, since it will keep discipline to a minimum and create a more positive learning environment for him. That, in turn, will also be easier on you!

Here are a few commonsense tips to keep your belongings safe and your puppy out of trouble:

Chow Chows are thoroughly confident of their own ability to be the leader of the pack and will be ready to assume that role if you abdicate your responsibilites.

- Keep your closet doors closed and your shoes, socks and other apparel off the floor so your puppy can't get at them.
- Keep a secure lid on the trash container or put the trash where your puppy can't dig into it. He can't damage what he can't reach!
- Supervise your puppy at all times to make sure he is not getting into mischief. If he starts to chew the corner of the rug, you can distract him instantly by tossing a toy for him to fetch. You also will be able to whisk him outside when you notice that he is about to piddle on the carpet. If you can't see your puppy, you can't teach or correct his behavior.

TEETHING TIME

All puppies chew. It's normal canine behavior. Chewing just plain feels good to a puppy, especially during the three- to five-month teething period when the adult teeth are breaking through the gums. Rather than attempting to eliminate such a strong natural chewing instinct, you will be more successful if you redirect it and teach your puppy what he may or may not chew. Correct inappropriate chewing with a sharp "No!" and offer him a chew toy, praising him when he takes it. Don't become discouraged. Chewing usually decreases after the adult teeth have come in.

SOLVING PUPPY PROBLEMS

CHEWING AND NIPPING

Nipping at fingers and toes is normal puppy behavior. Chewing is also the way that puppies investigate their surroundings. However, you will have to teach your puppy that chewing anything other than his toys is not acceptable. That won't happen overnight and at times puppy teeth will test your patience. However, if you allow nipping and chewing to continue, just think about the damage that a mature Chow can do with a full set of adult teeth.

Whenever your puppy nips your hand or fingers, cry out "Ouch!" in a loud voice, which should startle your puppy and stop him from nipping, even if only for a moment. Immediately distract him by offering a small treat or an appropriate toy for him to chew instead (which means having chew toys and puppy treats handy or in your pockets at all times). Praise him when he takes the toy and tell him what a good fellow he is. Praise is just as or even more important in puppy training as discipline and correction.

Puppies also tend to nip at children more often than adults, since they perceive little ones to be more vulnerable and more similar to their littermates. Teach your children appropriate

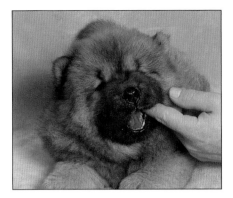

responses to nipping behavior. If they are unable to handle it themselves, you may have to intervene. Puppy nips can be quite painful and a child's frightened reaction will only encourage a puppy to nip harder, which is a natural canine response. As with all other puppy situations, interaction between your Chow puppy and children should be supervised.

Chewing on objects, not just family members' fingers and ankles, is also normal canine behavior that can be especially tedious (for the owner, not the pup) during the teething period when the puppy's adult teeth are coming in. At this stage, chewing just plain feels good. Furniture legs and cabinet corners are common puppy favorites. Shoes and other personal items also taste pretty good to a pup.

The best solution is, once again, prevention. If you value something, keep it tucked away and out of reach. You can't hide your dining-room table in a closet, but you can try to deflect the chewing by applying a bitter product made just to deter dogs from chewing. Available in a spray or cream, this substance is vile-tasting, although safe for dogs, and most puppies will avoid the forbidden object after one tiny taste. You also can apply the product to your leather leash if the puppy tries to chew on his lead during leash- training sessions.

Keep a ready supply of safe chews handy to offer your Chow as a distraction when he starts to chew on something that's a "no-no." Remember, at this tender age, he does not yet know what is permitted or forbidden, so you have to be "on call" every minute he's awake and on the prowl.

You may lose a treasure or two during puppy's growing-up period, and the furniture could sustain a nasty nick or two. These can be trying times, so be prepared for those inevitable accidents and comfort yourself in knowing that this too shall pass.

JUMPING UP

Although Chow pups are not known to be notorious jumpers, they are still puppies after all, and puppies jump up...on you, your guests, your counters and your furniture. Just another normal part of growing up, and one you need to meet head-on before it becomes an ingrained habit.

A finger makes a tasty treat for a teething pup! Nipping, however, should be discouraged, as it can lead to dangerous habits as the dog matures.

The key to jump correction is consistency. You cannot correct your Chow for jumping up on you today, then allow it to happen tomorrow by greeting him with hugs and kisses. As you have learned by now, consistency is critical to all puppy lessons.

For starters, try turning your back as soon as the puppy jumps. Jumping up is a means of gaining your attention and, if the pup can't see your face, he may get discouraged and learn that he loses eye contact with his beloved master when he jumps up.

Leash corrections also work, and most puppies respond well to a leash tug if they jump. Grasp the leash close to the puppy's collar and give a quick tug downward, using the command "Off." Do not use the word "Down," since "Down" is used to teach the puppy to lie down, which is a separate action that he will learn during his education in the basic commands. As soon as the puppy has backed off, tell him to sit and immediately praise him for doing so. This will take many repetitions and won't be accomplished quickly, so don't get discouraged or give up; you must be even more persistent than your puppy.

A second method used for jump correction is the spritzer bottle. Fill a spray bottle with water mixed with a bit of lemon juice or vinegar. As soon as puppy jumps, command him "Off" and spritz him with the water mixture. Of course, that means having the spray bottle handy whenever or wherever jumping usually happens.

Yet a third method to discourage jumping is grasping the puppy's paws and holding them gently but firmly until he struggles to get away. Wait a brief moment or two, then release his paws and give him a command to sit. He should eventually learn that jumping gets him into an uncomfortable predicament.

Children are major victims of puppy jumping, since puppies view little people as ready targets for jumping up as well as nipping. If your children (or their friends) are unable to dispense jump

DIGGING OUT

Some dogs love to dig. Others wouldn't think of it. Digging is considered "self-rewarding behavior" because it's fun! Of all the digging solutions offered by the experts, most are only marginally successful and none is guaranteed to work. The best cure is prevention, which means removing the dog from the offending site when he digs as well as distracting him when you catch him digging so that he turns his attentions elsewhere. That means that you have to supervise your dog's yard time. An unsupervised digger can create havoc with your landscaping or, worse, run away!

corrections, you will have to intervene and handle it for them.

Important to prevention is also knowing what you should not do. Never kick your Chow (for any reason, not just for jumping) or knock him in the chest with your knee. That maneuver could actually harm your puppy. Vets can tell you stories about puppies who suffered broken bones after being banged about when they jumped up.

PUPPY WHINING

Puppies often cry and whine, just as infants and little children do. It's their way of telling us that they are lonely or in need of attention. Your puppy will miss his littermates and will feel insecure when he is left alone. You may be out of the house or just in another room, but he will still feel alone. During these times, the puppy's crate should be his personal comfort station, a place all his own where he can feel safe and secure. Once he learns that being alone is okay and not something to be feared, he will settle down without crying or objecting. You might want to leave a radio on while he is crated, as the sound of human voices can be soothing and will give the impression that people are around.

Give your puppy a favorite cuddly toy or chew toy to entertain him whenever he is crated. You will both be happier: the puppy because he is safe in his den and you because he is quiet, safe and not getting into puppy escapades that can wreak havoc in your house or cause him danger.

To make sure that your puppy will always view his crate as a safe and cozy place, never, ever, use the crate as punishment. That's the best way to turn the crate into a negative place that the pup will want to avoid. Sure, you can use the crate for your own peace of mind if your puppy is getting into trouble and needs some "time out." Just don't let him know that! Never scold the pup and immediately place him into the crate. Count to ten, give him a couple of hugs and maybe a treat, then scoot him into his crate.

It's also important not to make a big fuss when he is released from the crate. That will make getting out of the crate more appealing than being in the crate, which is just the opposite of what you are trying to achieve.

FOOD GUARDING

Some dogs are picky eaters; others seem to inhale their food without chewing it. Occasionally the true "chow hound" will become protective of his food, which is one dangerous step toward other aggressive behavior. Food guarding is obvious: your puppy will growl, snarl or even attempt to bite you if you approach his food bowl or put your hand into his pan while he's eating.

This behavior is not acceptable, and very preventable! If your puppy is an especially voracious eater, sit next to him occasionally while he eats and dangle your fingers in his food bowl. Don't feed him in a corner, where he could feel possessive of his eating space. Rather, place his food bowl in an open area of your kitchen where you are in close proximity. Occasionally remove his food in mid-meal, tell him he's a good boy and return his bowl.

If your pup becomes possessive of his food, look for other signs of future aggression, like guarding his favorite toys or refusing to obey obedience commands that he knows. Consult an obedience trainer for help in reinforcing obedience so your Chow will fully understand that *you* are the boss.

DOMESTIC SQUABBLES

How well your new Chow will get along with an older dog who has squatter's rights depends largely on the individual dogs. Like people, some dogs are more gregarious than others and will enjoy having a furry friend to play with. Others will not be thrilled at the prospect of sharing their dog space with another canine.

It's best to introduce the dogs to each other on neutral ground, away from home, so the resident dog won't feel so possessive. Keep both puppy and adult on loose leads (loose is very important, as a tight lead sends negative signals and can intimidate either dog) and allow them to sniff and do their doggy things. A few raised hackles are normal, with the older dog pawing at the youngster. Let the two work things out between them unless you see signs of real aggression, such as deep growls or curled lips and serious snarls. You may have to keep them separated until the veteran gets used to the new family member, often after the pup has outgrown the silly puppy stage and is more mature in stature. Take precautions to make sure that the puppy does not become frightened by the older dog's behavior.

Whatever happens, it's important to make your resident dog feel secure. (Jealousy is normal among dogs, too!) Pay extra attention to the older dog: feed him first, hug him first and don't insist he share his toys or space with the new pup until he's ready. If the two are still at odds months later, consult an obedience professional for advice.

Cat introductions are easier, believe it or not. Being agile and independent creatures, cats will scoot to high places, out of the puppy's reach. A cat might even tease the puppy and cuff him from above when the pup comes within paw's reach. However, most will end up buddies if you just let dog-and-cat nature run its course.

PROPER CARE OF YOUR

CHOW CHOW

FEEDING YOUR CHOW CHOW

When you take your puppy home, it is normally around eight weeks of age, should have been carefully weaned, and will perhaps be on three meals per day. Whether you fully agree with the breeder's diet and feeding regimen, it is inadvisable to make sudden changes. After all, it will not have been so long since your puppy was feeding from its mother and will only have been weaned for perhaps three weeks. Your breeder will know which food is best suited, and how much is needed. If, at some time, you need or decide to make changes in the pup's diet, then the change should always be administered with the greatest care, and without haste. It is normal practice for caring breeders to advise on all aspects of the puppy's lifestyle, and they will invariably let you know what food to obtain beforehand. Some will actually ensure that there is some ready for you to take home. In days gone by, when plenty of fresh meat was obtainable at reasonable prices, we would normally feed that, mixed with

some good-quality biscuit meal. In more recent times, with the increased cost of fresh meat, more dog owners have moved over to the complete foods, while some prefer canned foods. The former comes in kibble or pellet form, and preferably should be moistened. If a dog was living wild, the food that it hunted would not be in a dry form, therefore I feel it is unfair to expect our dogs' digestions to adapt to unnatural nutrition.

When considering the purchase of any breed, the cost of feeding is something that should be taken into account. A growing dog will gradually need larger

Your Chow puppy will have to rely on you for a proper diet, so choose wisely.

may be special situations in which pups fail to nurse, necessitating that the breeder hand-feed them with a formula, but for the most part pups spend the first weeks of life nursing from their dam. The breeder weans the pups by gradually introducing solid foods and decreasing the milk meals. Pups may even start themselves off on the weaning process, albeit inadvertently, if they snatch bites from their mom's food bowl.

THE DARK SIDE OF CHOCOLATE

From a tiny chip to a giant rabbit, chocolate—in any form—is not your dog's friend. Whether it's an Oreo® cookie, a Snickers® bar or even a couple of M&M's®, you should avoid these items with your dog. You are also well advised to avoid any bone toy that is made out of fake chocolate or any treat made of carob—anything that encourages your dog to become a "chocoholic" can't be helpful. Before you toss your pooch half of your candy bar, consider that as little as a single ounce of chocolate can poison a 30-pound dog. Theobromine, like caffeine, is a methylxanthine and occurs naturally in cocoa beans. Dogs metabolize theobromine very slowly, and its effect on the dog can be serious, harming the heart, kidneys and central nervous system. Dark or semi-sweet chocolate is even worse than milk chocolate, and baking chocolate and cocoa mix are by far the worst.

Breeders introduce their pups to regular foods by weaning them off the nursing routine on a gradual basis. quantities, even though the number of feedings will eventually be reduced to one per day. We always fed our puppies a cereal-type breakfast, a light lunch and an evening meat and meal mixture. Today's complete foods are carefully formulated and will be graded according to needs: puppy, junior, adult, senior, etc. They are sold with details of amounts required according to size of breed and any preparation needs. The grading ensures that the balance of protein and carbohydrate is in keeping with growth stages.

FEEDING THE PUPPY
Of course, your pup's very first food will be his dam's milk. There

VARIETY IS THE SPICE

Although dog-food manufacturers contend that dogs don't like variety in their diets, studies show quite the opposite to be true. Dogs would much rather vary their meals than eat the same old chow day in and day out. Dry kibble is no more exciting for a dog than the same bowl of bran flakes would be for you. Fortunately, there are dozens of varieties available on the market, and your dog will likely show preference for certain flavors over others. A word of warning: don't overdo it or you'll develop a fussy eater who only prefers chopped beef fillet and asparagus tips every night.

By the time the pups are ready for new homes, they are fully weaned and eating a good puppy food. As a new owner, you may be thinking, "Great! The breeder has taken care of the hard part." Not so fast.

A puppy's first year of life is the time when all or most of his growth and development takes place. This is a delicate time, and diet plays a huge role in proper skeletal and muscular formation. Improper diet and exercise habits can lead to damaging problems that will compromise the dog's health and movement for his entire life. That being said, new owners should not worry needlessly. With the myriad types of food formulated specifically for growing pups of different-sized breeds, dog-food manufacturers have taken much of the guesswork out of feeding your puppy well. Since growth-food formulas are designed to provide the nutrition that a growing puppy needs, it is unnecessary and, in fact, can prove harmful to add supplements to the diet. Research has shown that too much of certain vitamin supplements and minerals predis-

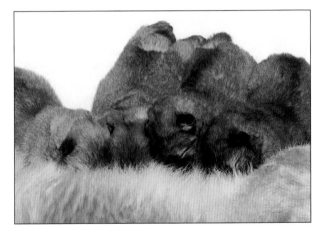

pose a dog to skeletal problems. It's by no means a case of "if a little is good, a lot is better." At every stage of your dog's life, too much or too little in the way of nutrients can be harmful, which is why a manufactured complete food is the easiest way to know that your dog is getting what he needs.

Because of a young pup's small body and accordingly small digestive system, his daily portion will be divided up into small

There is nothing more nourishing and beneficial than mother's milk for newborn puppies.

FREE FEEDING

Many owners opt to feed their dogs the free way. That is, they serve dry kibble in a feeder that is available to the dog all day. Arguably, this is the most convenient method of feeding an adult dog, but it may encourage the dog to become fussy about food or defensive over his bowl. Free feeding is an option only for adult dogs, not puppies.

meals throughout the day. This can mean starting off with three or more meals a day and decreasing the number of meals as the pup matures. Eventually you can feed only one meal a day, although it is generally thought that dividing the day's food into two meals on a morning/evening schedule is healthier for the dog's digestion.

Regarding the feeding schedule, feeding the pup at the same times and in the same place each day is important for both housebreaking purposes and establishing the dog's everyday routine. As for the amount to feed, growing puppies generally need proportionately more food per body weight than their adult counterparts, but a pup should never be allowed to gain excess weight. Dogs of all ages should be kept in proper body condition, but extra weight can strain a pup's developing frame, causing skeletal problems.

Watch your pup's weight as he grows and, if the recommended amounts seem to be too much or too little for your pup, consult the vet about appropriate dietary changes. Keep in mind that treats, although small, can quickly add up throughout the day, contributing unnecessary calories. Treats are fine when used prudently; opt for dog treats specially formulated to be healthy or for nutritious snacks like small pieces of cheese or cooked chicken.

FEEDING THE ADULT DOG

For the adult (meaning physically mature) dog, feeding properly is about maintenance, not growth. Again, correct weight is a concern. Your dog should appear fit and should have an evident "waist." His ribs should not be protruding (a sign of being underweight), but they should be covered by only a slight layer of fat. Under normal circumstances, an adult dog can be maintained fairly easily with a high-quality nutritionally complete adult-formula food.

Factor treats into your dog's overall daily caloric intake, and avoid offering table scraps. Over-weight dogs are more prone to health problems. Research has even shown that obesity takes years off a dog's life. With that in mind, resist the urge to overfeed and over-treat. Don't make unnecessary additions to your dog's diet, whether with tidbits

Stainless steel food and water vessels are relatively easy to keep clean, an important consideration in your choice of feeding implements.

or with extra vitamins and minerals.

The amount of food needed for proper maintenance will vary depending on the individual dog's activity level, but you will be able to tell whether the daily portions are keeping him in good shape. With the wide variety of good complete foods available, choosing what to feed is largely a matter of personal preference. Just as with the puppy, the adult dog should have consistency in his mealtimes and feeding place. In addition to a consistent routine, regular mealtimes also allow the owner to see how much his dog is eating. If the dog seems never to be satisfied or, likewise, becomes uninterested in his food, the owner will know right away that something is wrong and can consult the vet.

DIETS FOR THE AGING DOG

A good rule of thumb is that once a dog has reached 75% of his

---

HOLD THE ONIONS

Sliced, chopped, grated; dehydrated, boiled, fried or raw; pearl, Spanish, white or red: onions can be deadly to your dog. The toxic effects of onions in dogs are cumulative for up to 30 days. A serious form of anemia, called Heinz body anemia, affects the red blood cells of dogs that have eaten onions. For safety (and better breath), dogs should avoid chives and scallions as well.

What does aging have to do with your dog's diet? No, he won't get a discount at the local diner's early-bird special. Yes, he will require some dietary changes to accommodate the changes that come along with increased age. One change is that the older dog's dietary needs become more similar to that of a puppy. Specifically, dogs can metabolize more protein as youngsters and seniors than in the adult-maintenance stage. Discuss with your vet whether you need to switch to a higher-protein or senior-formulated food or whether your current adult-dog food contains sufficient nutrition for the senior.

The Chow has a broad muzzle and therefore should be provided with bowls that are not too narrow.

expected lifespan, he has reached "senior citizen" or geriatric status. Your Chow will be considered a senior at about 8 years of age; based on his size, he has a projected lifespan of about 12 years.

Watching the dog's weight remains essential, even more so in the senior stage. Older dogs are

All Chows, puppies and adults, must always have fresh, clean water available.

already more vulnerable to illness, and obesity only contributes to their susceptibility to problems. As the older dog becomes less active and thus exercises less, his regular portions may cause him to gain weight. At this point, you may consider decreasing his daily food intake or switching to a reduced-calorie food. As with other changes, you should consult your vet for advice.

Don't Forget the Water!

For a dog, it's always time for a drink! Regardless of what type of food he eats, there's no doubt that he needs plenty of water. Fresh cold water, in a clean bowl, should be freely available to your dog at all times. There are special circumstances, such as during puppy housebreaking, when you will want to monitor your pup's water intake so that you will be able to predict when he will need to relieve himself, but water must be available to him nonetheless. Water is essential for hydration and proper body function just as it is in humans.

You will get to know how much your dog typically drinks in a day. Of course, in the heat or if exercising vigorously, he will be more thirsty and will drink more. However, if he begins to drink noticeably more water for no apparent reason, this could signal any of various problems, and you are advised to consult your vet.

Daily walks are equally beneficial for dogs and their owners.

Water is the best drink for dogs. Some owners are tempted to give milk from time to time or to moisten dry food with milk, but dogs do not have the enzymes necessary to digest the lactose in milk, which is much different from the milk that nursing puppies receive. Therefore stick with clean fresh water to quench your dog's thirst, and always have it readily available to him.

EXERCISE

The Chow Chow who is involved in the family activities is twice blessed. Providing the Chow with active participation in outdoor endeavors allows for exercise as well as social stimulation. The best exercise for a Chow involves his owner, other members of the family or familiar friends. The Chow cannot be permitted to lead

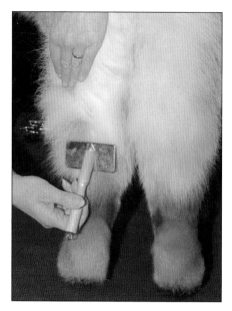

The Chow is a natural breed, meaning that its coat needs no special clipping or trimming. Regular brushing is enough to keep the Chow's coat in good condition.

a sedentary lifestyle. Not only is this unhealthy for any dog, but for a Chow, lack of exercise and social outings makes him a recluse, totally uninterested in other life forms. Many Chows are self-sufficient and aloof, rarely looking for company and play.

Exercise and play are vital to all dogs, and the Chow is a special case indeed. Regular walks, fetching balls in the yard, or letting the dog run free in the yard under your supervision are excellent outings for the Chow. For those who are more ambitious, you will find that your Chow also enjoys long walks, an occasional hike or a trip to the beach. Family picnics, dog show weekends, road trips and the like are ideal, as they offer the Chow

opportunities to engage in social exchanges, ever increasing the dog's ability to "let his ruff down" and let his charming leonine personality "roar"!

GROOMING

It is important to remember that the Chow is a natural breed that requires no clipping or trimming outside of tidying up its feet or removing the whiskers. Breeders are most adamant that the Chow not fall into any grooming fads of any kind. Proper brushing is all the grooming that your Chow will ever need.

PUPPY COAT

Undoubtedly the breeder from whom you bought your Chow will have begun to accustom the puppy to grooming as soon as there was enough hair to brush. You must continue with grooming sessions or begin them at once if for some reason they have not been started. You and your Chow will spend many hours involved with this activity over a lifetime, so it is imperative you both learn to cooperate in the endeavor to make it an easy and pleasant experience.

The first piece of equipment you will have to obtain is a grooming table. A grooming table can be built or purchased at your local pet shop. Make sure the table is of a height at which you can work comfortably either sitting or standing. Adjustable-height grooming tables are available at most pet shops. Although you will buy this when your Chow puppy first arrives, anticipate the dog's full-grown size in making your purchase and select or build a table that will accommodate a full-grown Chow lying on its side.

You will also need to invest in two brushes, a steel comb, barber's scissors and a pair of nail

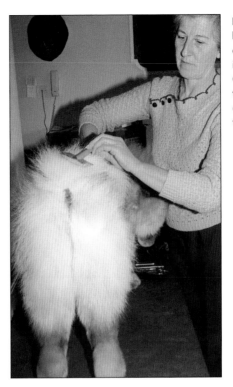

Hair should be brushed in the direction in which it falls. With the Chow, the hair on the tail naturally curls over the back.

SCOOTING HIS BOTTOM

Here's a doggy problem that many owners tend to neglect. If your dog is scooting his rear end around the carpet, he probably is experiencing anal-sac impaction or blockage. The anal sacs are the two grape-sized glands on either side of the dog's vent. The dog cannot empty these glands, which become filled with a foul-smelling material. The dog may attempt to lick the area to relieve the pressure. He may also rub his anus on your walls, furniture or floors.

Don't neglect your dog's rear end during grooming sessions. By squeezing both sides of the anus with a soft cloth, you can express some of the material in the sacs. If the material is pasty and thick, you likely will need the assistance of a veterinarian. Vets know how to express the glands and can show you how to do it correctly without hurting the dog or spraying yourself with poop.

clippers. For the finish work you will need a commercial coat conditioner and a spray bottle. Consider the fact you will be using this equipment for many years, so buy the best of these items that you can afford. The two brushes that you will need are a wire "slicker brush" (also called a "rake") and a pin brush (sometimes called a "Poodle brush").

Do not attempt to groom your Chow on the floor. The puppy will only attempt to get away from you when it has decided enough is enough, and you will spend a good part of your time chasing the

Shorter hair on the Chow's legs can be sufficiently maintained with a metal comb.

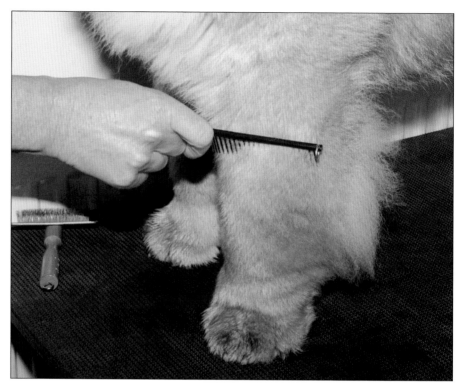

puppy around the room. Nor is sitting on the floor for long stretches of time the most comfortable position in the world for the average adult.

The Chow puppy must be taught to lie on its side to be groomed. It will be kept in that position for most of the grooming process. The puppy will also have to be kept in the sitting and standing position, but the lying position takes the most time and is more difficult for the puppy to learn. The Chow trained to lie quietly on its side will prove to be a true godsend when the dog is grown and has developed a mature coat.

Begin this training by picking the puppy up as you would a lamb with its side against your chest and your arms wrapped around the puppy's body. Lay the puppy down on the table; release your arms but keep your chest pressed lightly down on the puppy's side. Speak reassuringly to the Chow, stroking its head and rump. (This is a good time to practice the "Stay" command.) Do this a number of times before you attempt to do any grooming. Repeat the process until your puppy understands what it is supposed to do when you place it on the grooming table.

Start with the slicker brush and begin what is called "line-brushing" at the top of the shoulder. Part the hair in a straight line from the front of the shoulder straight on down to the bottom of the chest. Brush through the hair to the right and left of the part, lightly spraying the area with the coat conditioner as you go. Start at the skin and brush out to the very end of the hair. Do a small section at a time and continue on down the part. When you reach the bottom of the part, return to the top and make another part just to the right of the first line you brushed. Part, brush and spray. You will repeat this process working toward the rear until you reach the puppy's tail.

I prefer to do the legs on the same side I have been working on at this time. Use the same process, parting the hair at the top of the leg and working down. Do this all around the leg and be especially careful to attend to the hard-to-reach areas under the upper legs where they join the body. Mats occur in these areas very rapidly, especially during the time when the Chow is casting its puppy coat.

Should you encounter a mat that does not brush out easily, use your fingers and the steel comb to separate the hairs as much as possible. Do not cut or pull out

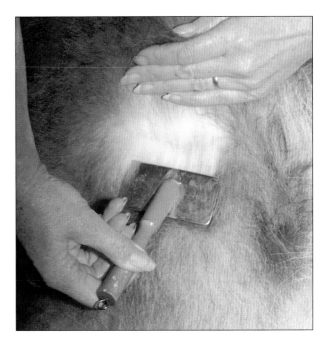

the matted hair. Apply baby powder or one of the specially prepared grooming powders directly to the mat and brush completely from the skin out.

When you have finished the legs on the one side, turn the puppy over and complete the entire process, on the other side—part, spray, brush. As your Chow becomes accustomed to this process, you may find the puppy considers this nap time. You may have to lift your puppy into sitting position to arouse it from its slumber.

While the puppy is sitting, you can do the hair of the chest using the line-brushing method here as well. Next stand the

Learn the correct way to brush your Chow's coat and make regular grooming a habit.

Scissoring around the Chow's feet to give them a neat look is about all the trimming that the Chow's coat requires.

puppy up and do the tail. Check the longer hair of the "pants" on the rear legs to make sure they are thoroughly brushed, especially around the area of the anus and genitalia. Needless to say, it is important to be extremely careful when brushing in these areas in that they are extremely sensitive and easily injured.

When the line-brushing process is completed, it is time for

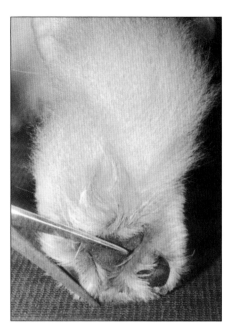

GROOMING TIP

Although grooming the pet Chow might seem like a daunting task, it is possible to do it yourself. Watch a professional work on your dog a few times and then practice yourself.

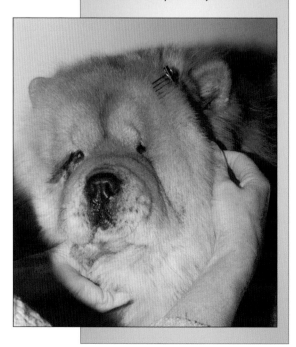

the finishing touches. Use your barber scissors to trim any long or shaggy hairs around the Chow's feet. The Chow's foot should be round and compact-looking. You may trim off your Chow's whiskers if you wish. This is optional, however. Many Chow owners prefer to leave the whiskers on.

Brush the hair around the head, shoulders and on the back forward. Do the same with the hair on the tail. Brush the chest hair downward and do the same with the hair on the sides of the dog.

This is also a good time to accustom your Chow to having its nails trimmed and having its feet inspected. Always inspect your dog's feet for cracked pads. Check between the toes for splinters and thorns. Pay particular attention to any swollen or tender areas. In many sections of the world, there is a weed called a "fishtail" that has a barbed hook-like affair that carries its seed. This hook easily finds its way into a Chow's foot or between its toes and very quickly works its way deep into the dog's flesh. This will very quickly cause soreness and infection. Fishtails are best removed by your vet before serious problems develop.

The nails of a Chow who spends most of its time indoors or on grass when outdoors can grow long very quickly. Do not allow the nails to become overgrown and then expect to cut them back easily. Each nail has a blood vessel called the "quick" running through the center. The quick grows close to the end of the nail and contains very sensitive nerve endings. If the nail is allowed to grow too long, it will be impossible to cut it back to a proper length without cutting into the quick. This causes severe pain to the dog and can also result in a great deal of bleeding that can be very difficult to stop.

If your Chow is getting plenty of exercise on cement or rough, hard pavement, the nails may keep sufficiently worn down. Otherwise the nails can grow long very quickly. They must then be trimmed with canine nail clip-

pers, an electric nail grinder or coarse file made expressly for that purpose. All three of these items can be purchased at well-stocked pet shops.

The electric nail grinder is preferred above the others because

THE MONTHLY GRIND

If your dog doesn't like the feeling of nail clippers or if you're not comfortable using them, you may wish to try an electric nail grinder. This tool has a small sandpaper disc on the end that rotates to grind the nails down. Some feel that using a grinder reduces the risk of cutting into the quick; this can be true if the tool is used properly. Usually you will be able to tell where the quick is before you get to it. A benefit of the grinder is that it creates a smooth finish on the nails so that there are no ragged edges.

Because the tool makes noise, your dog should be introduced to it before the actual grinding takes place. Turn it on and let your dog hear the noise; turn it off and let him inspect it with you holding it. Use the grinder gently, holding it firmly and progressing a little at a time until you reach the proper length. Look at the nail as you grind so that you do not go too short. Stop at any indication that you are nearing the quick. It will take a few sessions for both you and the puppy to get used to the grinder. Make sure that you don't let his hair get tangled in the grinder.

The puppy's coat hardly resembles the full plush coat of the adult, though still requires brushing to keep clean and mat free.

Use of the electric grinder requires introducing your puppy to it at an early age. The instrument has a whining sound to it not unlike a dentist's drill. The noise combined with the vibration of the sanding head on the nail itself can take some getting used to, but most dogs I have used it on eventually accept it as one of life's trials. Most dogs do not like having their nails trimmed no matter which device is used, so my own eventual decision was to use the grinder, as I was less likely to damage the quick.

Should the quick be nipped in the trimming process, there are any number of blood-clotting products available that will almost immediately stem the flow of blood. It is wise to have one of these products on hand in case there is a nail-trimming accident or the dog tears a nail on its own.

it is so easy to control and helps avoid cutting into the quick. The Chow's dark nails make it practically impossible to see where the quick ends, so regardless of which nail-trimming device is used, one must proceed with caution and remove only a small portion of the nail at time.

GROOMING THE ADULT CHOW
Fortunately, you and your Chow have spent the many months between puppyhood and full maturity learning to assist each other through the grooming process. The two of you have survived the casting of the puppy coat and the arrival of the entirely different adult hair. Not only is the Chow's adult hair of an entirely different texture, it is much longer and much thicker.

Undoubtedly by this time you have realized the pin brush with

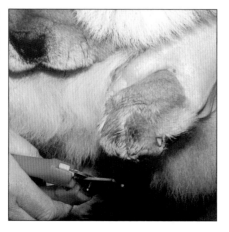

Adult nails will be thicker than puppy nails and will require a stronger clipper.

its longer bristles set in rubber is far more effective for line-brushing the adult Chow than the slicker brush that you used through puppyhood. The method of brushing the adult coat is the same as that used since your Chow was a puppy. The obvious difference is that you have more dog and more hair.

While one might expect grooming an adult Chow to be a monumental task, this is not necessarily so. The two of you have been practicing the brushing routine for so long it has undoubtedly become second nature to both of you. The coarseness of the adult Chow's hair is actually much easier to cope with than was the puppy coat. The ease of working with the Chow's adult coat plus your own experience in the grooming routine combine to make the task far easier than what one might expect. Ten industriously applied minutes a day with a brush, in addition to a thorough weekly session, will keep your Chow looking in the best of shape.

On the other hand, if the coat is neglected and becomes matted, you will indeed have a difficult time ahead of you. The coat can become "felted" with mats and you may have to resort to having a vet or groomer shave the matted-to-the-skin Chow. This should be resorted to only under extreme circumstances. Some misguided

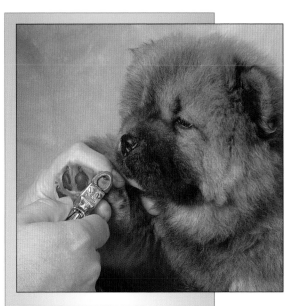

NAIL MAINTENANCE
It is best to get your dog accustomed to this procedure at an early age so that he is used to it. Some dogs are especially sensitive about having their feet touched, but if a dog has experienced it since he was young, he should not be bothered by it. A dog that spends a lot of time outside on a hard surface, such as cement or pavement, will have his nails naturally worn down and may not need to have them trimmed as often, except maybe in the colder months when he is not outside as much.

owners feel they are doing their dog a service by shaving the coat in summer when exactly the opposite is true. The Chow's coat serves as insulation against both heat and cold.

BATHING

Following the proper coat care procedure will all but eliminate the need for bathing a Chow. Dog show exhibitors use coat care products that adhere to the Chow's hair and may make bathing necessary on occasion. Even at that, most Chow exhibitors use "dry bath" products rather than the tub and shampoo method. Well-kept Chows are literally odor-free and frequent bathing serves little purpose. Bathing can dry out the Chow's skin and hair, creating unnecessary problems.

If you must bathe your Chow never bathe him while he is matted. Wetting the matted hair will only complicate the situation and the end result will provide you with much more work than if you had completed the mat-removal process prior to bathing. On the rare occasions your Chow requires a wet bath, you will need to gather the necessary equipment ahead of time.

A rubber mat should be placed at the bottom of the tub to avoid your Chow's slipping and thereby becoming frightened. A rubber spray hose is absolutely necessary to thoroughly wet the Chow's dense coat. The hose is also necessary to remove all shampoo residue.

A small piece of cotton placed inside each ear will avoid water running down into the dog's ear canal and a drop or two of mineral oil or a dab of petroleum jelly placed in each eye will preclude shampoo from irritating the Chow's eyes.

It is best to use a shampoo designed especially for dogs. The pH balance is adjusted to keep drying to a minimum and leaves the hair shining and lustrous.

In bathing, start behind the ears and work back. Use a face flannel to soap and rinse around the head and face. Once you have shampooed your Chow, you must

WATER SHORTAGE

No matter how well behaved your dog is, bathing is always a project! Nothing can substitute for a good warm bath, but owners do have the option of giving their dogs "dry" baths. Pet shops sell excellent products, in both powder and spray forms, designed for spot-cleaning your dog. These dry shampoos are convenient for touch-up jobs when you don't have the time to bathe your dog in the traditional way.

Muddy feet, messy behinds and smelly coats can be spot-cleaned and deodorized with a "wet-nap"-style cleaner. On those days when your dog insists on rolling in fresh goose droppings and there's no time for a bath, a spot bath can save the day. These pre-moistened wipes are also handy for other grooming needs like wiping faces, ears and eyes and freshening tails and behinds.

rinse the coat thoroughly and when you feel quite certain all shampoo residue has been removed, rinse once more. Shampoo residue in the coat is sure to dry the hair and could cause skin irritation.

As soon as you have completed the bath, use heavy towels to remove as much of the excess water as possible. Your Chow will assist you in the process by shaking a great deal of the water out of its coat on its own.

Before your Chow is completely dry, it is best to brush out the coat to avoid mats and tangles from forming. Use the same brushing process you normally use.

My advice is to avoid the wet bath unless it is absolutely necessary. There are so many effective dry bath products available that the time-consuming wet bath need be resorted to only in extreme circumstances.

EAR CLEANING

While keeping your dog's ears clean unfortunately will not cause him to "hear" your commands any better, it will protect him from ear infection and ear-mite infestation. In addition, a dog's ears are vulnerable to waxy build-up and to collecting foreign matter from the outdoors. Look in your dog's ears regularly to ensure that they look pink, clean and

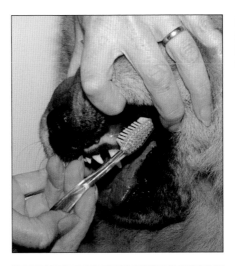

Part of good grooming is brushing your dog's teeth.

The areas around the eyes can be wiped with a special cleaner formulated for dogs.

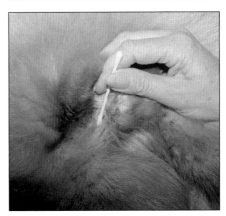

Your Chow's ears should be cleaned very carefully. Probing with a cotton bud is not advised; a cotton wipe is much safer.

otherwise healthy. Even if they look fine, an odor in the ears signals a problem and means it's time to call the vet.

A dog's ears should be cleaned regularly; once a week is suggested, and you can do this along with your regular brushing. Using a cotton ball or pad, and never probing into the ear canal, wipe the ear gently. You can use an ear-cleansing liquid or powder available from your vet or pet-supply store; alternatively, you might prefer to use home-made solutions with ingredients like one part white vinegar and one part hydrogen peroxide. Ask your vet about home remedies before you attempt to concoct something on your own!

Keep your dog's ears free of excess hair by plucking it as needed. If done gently, this will be painless for the dog. Look for wax, brown droppings (a sign of ear mites), redness or any other abnormalities. At the first sign of a problem, contact your vet so that he can prescribe an appropriate medication.

IDENTIFICATION AND TRAVEL

ID FOR YOUR DOG
You love your Chow and want to keep him safe. Of course you take every precaution to prevent his escaping from the yard or becoming lost or stolen. You have a sturdy high fence and you always keep your dog on lead when out and about in public places. If your dog is not properly identified, however, you are overlooking a major aspect of his safety. We hope to never be in a situation where our dog is missing, but we should practice prevention in the unfortunate case that this happens; identification greatly increases the chances of your dog's being returned to you

There are several ways to identify your dog. First, the traditional dog tag should be a staple in your dog's wardrobe, attached to his everyday collar. Tags can be made of sturdy plastic and various metals and should include your contact information so that a person who finds the dog can get in touch with you right away to arrange his return. Many people today enjoy the wide range of decorative tags available, so have fun and create a tag to match your dog's personality. Of course, it is

If you plan to travel with your Chow Chow, whether by automobile or a public conveyance that accepts dogs, you should make certain that he bears a permanent identification.

Your Chow must be transported in his crate or cage. Never allow the dog to roam free in the car while traveling. Imagine the turmoil if you have to stop short!

important that the tag stays on the collar, so have a secure "O" ring attachment; you also can explore the type of tag that slides right onto the collar.

In addition to the ID tag, which every dog should wear even if identified by another method, two other forms of identification have become popular: microchipping and tattooing. In microchipping, a tiny scannable chip is painlessly inserted under the dog's skin. The number is registered to you so that, if your lost dog turns up at a clinic or shelter, the chip can be scanned to retrieve your contact information.

The advantage of the microchip is that it is a permanent form of ID, but there are some factors to consider. Several different companies make microchips, and not all are compatible with the others' scanning devices. It's best to find a company with a universal microchip that can be read by scanners made by other companies as well. It won't do any good to have the dog chipped if the information cannot be retrieved. Also, not every humane society, shelter and clinic is equipped with a scanner, although more and more facilities are equipping

and veterinary clinics offer this service, which is usually very affordable.

Though less popular than microchipping, tattooing is another permanent method of ID for dogs. Most vets perform this service, and there are also clinics that perform dog tattooing. This is also an affordable procedure and one that will not cause much discomfort for the dog. It is best to put the tattoo in a visible area, such as the ear, to deter theft. It is sad to say that there are cases of dogs' being stolen and sold to research laboratories, but such laboratories will not accept tattooed dogs.

To ensure that the tattoo is effective in aiding your dog's return to you, the tattoo number must be registered with a national organization. That way, when someone finds a tattooed dog a phone call to the registry will quickly match the dog with his owner.

Puppies left to their own devices in open yards can easily stray and get lost, making reliable identification all the more necessary.

themselves. In fact, many shelters microchip dogs that they adopt out to new homes.

In the US, there are five or six major microchip manufacturers as well as a few databases. The American Kennel Club's Companion Animal Recovery unit works in conjunction with HomeAgain™ Companion Animal Retrieval System (Schering-Plough). In the UK, The Kennel Club is affiliated with the National Pet Register, operated by Wood Green Animal Shelters.

Because the microchip is not visible to the eye, the dog must wear a tag that states that he is microchipped so that whoever picks him up will know to have him scanned. He of course also should have a tag with contact information in case his chip cannot be read. Humane societies

HIT THE ROAD
Car travel with your Chow may be limited to necessity only, such as trips to the vet, or you may bring your dog along almost everywhere you go. This will depend much on your individual dog and how he reacts to rides in the car. You can begin desensitizing your dog to car travel as a pup so that it's something that he's used to. Still, some dogs

suffer from motion sickness. Your vet may prescribe a medication for this if trips in the car pose a problem for your dog. At the very least, you will need to get him to the vet, so he will need to tolerate these trips with the least amount of hassle possible.

Start taking your pup on short trips, maybe just around the block to start. If he is fine with short trips, lengthen your rides a little at a time. Start to take him on your errands or just for drives around town. By this time it will be easy to tell whether your dog is a born traveler or would prefer staying at home when you are on the road.

Of course, safety is a concern for dogs in the car. First, he must travel securely, not left loose to roam about the car where he could be injured or distract the driver. A young pup can be held by a passenger initially but should soon graduate to a travel crate, which can be the same crate he uses in the home. Other options include a car harness (like a seat belt for dogs) and partitioning the back of the car with a gate made for this purpose.

Bring along what you will need for the dog. He should wear his collar and ID tags, of course, and you should bring his leash, water (and food if a long trip) and clean-up materials for potty breaks and in case of motion

sickness. Always keep your dog on his leash when you make stops, and never leave him alone in the car. Many a dog has died from the heat inside a closed car; this does not take much time at all. A dog left alone inside a car can also be a target for thieves.

DON'T LEAVE HOME WITHOUT IT!

For long trips, there's no doubt that the crate is the safest way to travel with your dog. Luckily, there are some other options for owners who can't accommodate a crate in their cars or whose dogs prove exceptionally difficult to crate-train. In some states, seatbelts are mandatory for humans, and you can consider using the seatbelt on your dog. Purchase a safety harness made for passenger pooches and pull your car's seatbelt through the loop on the harness.

For smaller dogs, consider a car seat made especially for canine passengers. Equipped with their own seatbelts, car seats attach to the seat of the car with the seatbelt.

Larger dogs can be restrained in the rear of the vehicle with a barrier, which you can purchase from a pet store or pet-supply outlet. The barrier is constructed of aluminum, steel or mesh netting. While this device will keep the dog in a designated area, it will not protect him from being jostled about the vehicle on a bumpy ride.

CHOW CHOW

You have not selected the Chow Chow because the breed is easy to train. On the contrary, the Chow Chow's reputation for obedience is sketchy at best, horrible at worst. Not unlike his Nordic cousins, the Spitz breeds, huskies and lapphunds, the Chow Chow can be difficult to convince to obey you. Chows are not like spaniels who live to please you or like hounds who will sell their souls for a chunk of cheese. Chows have dignity, Chows have philosophies, Chows have brains (which they store in rather thick skulls!).

The owner's approach to training the Chow Chow, however, is no different from training the more responsive breeds—it just requires more persistence, patience and good humor. Many Chows have been trained to perform complicated obedience tasks and excel in many kinds of trials—obedience, agility and beyond. No trainer doubts the intelligence of the Chow, but many would prefer not to have their techniques put to the test by a pig-headed, lion-faced, canine demigod!

BASIC TRAINING PRINCIPLES: PUPPY VS. ADULT

There's a big difference between training an adult dog and training a young puppy. With a young puppy, everything is new. At eight to ten weeks of age, he will be experiencing many things, and he has nothing with which to

THE RIGHT START

The best advice for a potential dog owner is to start with the very best puppy that money can buy. Don't shop around for a bargain in the newspaper. You're buying a companion, not a used Buick or a second-hand Maytag. The purchase price of the dog represents a very significant part of the investment, but this is indeed a very small sum compared to the expenses of maintaining the dog in good health. If you purchase a well-bred healthy and sound puppy, you will be starting right. An unhealthy puppy can cost you thousands of dollars in unnecessary veterinary expenses and, possibly, a fortune in heartbreak as well.

compare these experiences. Up to this point, he has been with his dam and littermates, not one-on-one with people except in his interactions with his breeder and visitors to the litter.

When you first bring the puppy home, he is eager to please you. This means that he accepts doing things your way. During the next couple of months, he will absorb the basis of everything he needs to know for the rest of his life. This early age is even referred to as the "sponge" stage. After that, for the next 18 months, it's up to you to reinforce good

manners by building on the foundation that you've established. Once your puppy is reliable in basic commands and behavior and has reached the appropriate age, you may gradually introduce him to some of the interesting sports, games and activities available to pet owners and their dogs.

Raising your puppy is a family affair. Each member of the family must know what rules to set forth for the puppy and how to use the same one-word commands to mean exactly the same thing every time. Even if yours is a large family, one person will soon be

Chows are challenging dogs to train. Of course they are trainable, but one has to take the breed's unique personality into account when considering the approach to training.

Adopting an adult dog instead of a puppy can save you from certain house-training duties, but only if you're certain that the dog you acquire has itself been properly house-trained.

considered by the pup to be the leader, the Alpha person in his pack, the "boss" who must be obeyed. Often that highly regarded person turns out to be the one who feeds the puppy. Food ranks very high on the puppy's list of important things! That's why your puppy is rewarded with small treats along with verbal praise when he responds to you correctly. As the puppy learns to do what you want him to do, the food rewards are gradually eliminated and only the praise remains. If you were to keep up with the food treats, you could have two problems on your hands—an obese dog and a beggar.

Training begins the minute your Chow puppy steps through the doorway of your home, so don't make the mistake of putting the puppy on the floor and telling him by your actions to "Go for it! Run wild!" Even if this is your first puppy, you must act as if you know what you're doing: be the boss. An uncertain pup may be terrified to move, while a bold one will be ready to take you at your word and start plotting to destroy the house! Before you collected your puppy, you decided where his own special place would be, and that's where to put him when you first arrive home. Give him a house tour after he has investigated his area and had a nap and a bathroom "pit stop."

It's worth mentioning here that, if you've adopted an adult dog that is completely trained to your liking, lucky you! You're off the hook! However, if that dog spent his life up to this point in a kennel, or even in a good home but without any real training, be prepared to tackle the job ahead. A dog three years of age or older with no previous training cannot be blamed for not knowing what he was never taught. While the dog is trying to understand and learn your rules, at the same time he has to unlearn many of his previously self-taught habits and general view of the world.

Working with a professional trainer will speed up your

progress with an adopted adult dog. You'll need patience, too. Some new rules may be close to impossible for the dog to accept. After all, he's been successful so far by doing everything his way! (Patience again.) He may agree with your instruction for a few days and then slip back into his old ways, so you must be just as consistent and understanding in your teaching as you would be with a puppy. (More patience needed yet again!) Your dog has to learn to pay attention to your voice, your family, the daily routine, new smells, new sounds and, in some cases, even a new climate.

One of the most important things to find out about a newly adopted adult dog is his reaction to children (yours and others), strangers and your friends, and

how he acts upon meeting other dogs. If he was not socialized with dogs as a puppy, this could be a major problem. This does not mean that he's a "bad" dog, a vicious dog or an aggressive dog; rather, it means that he has no idea how to read another dog's body language. There's no way for him to tell whether the other dog is a friend or foe. Survival instinct takes over, telling him to attack first and ask questions later. This definitely calls for professional help and, even then, may not be a behavior that can be corrected 100% reliably (or even at all). If you have a puppy, this is why it is so very important to introduce your young puppy properly to other puppies and "dog-friendly" adult dogs.

What goes in … must come out. Adults have complete control of their bladders, an ability that young puppies unfortunately (for owners) lack.

HOUSE-TRAINING YOUR CHOW
Dogs are tactility-oriented when it comes to house-training. In other words, they respond to the surface on which they are given approval

THE BEST INVESTMENT
Obedience school is as important for you and your dog as grammar school is for your kids, and it's a lot more fun! Don't shun classes thinking that your dog might embarrass you. He might! Instructors don't expect you to know everything, but they'll teach you the correct way to teach your dog so he won't embarrass you again. He'll become a social animal as you learn with other people and dogs. Home training, while effective in teaching your dog the basic commands, excludes these socialization benefits.

You can start out with paper-training indoors and switch over to an outdoor surface as the puppy matures and gains control over his need to eliminate. For the nay-sayers, don't worry—this won't mean that the dog will soil on every piece of newspaper lying around the house. You are training him to go outside, remember? Starting out by paper-training often is the only choice for a city dog.

WHEN YOUR PUPPY'S "GOT TO GO"
Your puppy's need to relieve himself is seemingly non-stop, but signs of improvement will be seen each week. From 8 to 10 weeks old, the puppy will have to be taken outside every time he wakes up, about 10-15 minutes after every meal and after every period of play—all day long,

Unless it's an emergency (aka the puppy is leaking), do not carry him outside. It's better to attach his leash and walk him to his relief area.

to eliminate. The choice is yours (the dog's version is in parentheses): The lawn (including the neighbors' lawns)? A bare patch of earth under a tree (where people like to sit and relax in the summertime)? Concrete steps or patio (all sidewalks, garage and basement floors)? The curbside (watch out for cars)? A small area of crushed stone in a corner of the yard (mine!)? The latter is the best choice if you can manage it, because it will remain strictly for the dog's use and is easy to keep clean.

> **CREATURES OF HABIT**
> Canine behaviorists and trainers aptly describe dogs as "creatures of habit," meaning that dogs respond to structure in their daily lives and welcome a routine. Do not interpret this to mean that dogs enjoy endless repetition in their training sessions. Dogs get bored just as humans do. Keep training sessions interesting and exciting. Vary the commands and the locations in which you practice. Give short breaks for play in between lessons. A bored student will never be the best performer in the class.

SOMEBODY TO BLAME

House-training a puppy can be frustrating for the puppy and the owner alike. The puppy does not instinctively understand the difference between defecating on the pavement outside and on the ceramic tile in the kitchen. He is confused and frightened by his human's exuberant reactions to his natural urges. The owner, arguably the more intelligent of the duo, is also frustrated that he cannot convince his puppy to obey his commands and instructions.

In frustration, the owner may struggle with the temptation to discipline the puppy, scold him or even strike him on the rear end. Shouting and smacking the puppy may make you feel better, but it will defeat your purpose in gaining your puppy's trust and respect. Don't blame your nine-week-old puppy. Blame yourself for not being 100% consistent in the puppy's lessons and routine. The lesson here is simple: try harder and your puppy will succeed.

If that seems overwhelming or impossible, do a little planning. For example, plan to pick up your puppy at the start of a vacation period. If you can't get home in the middle of the day, plan to hire a dog-sitter or ask a neighbor to come over to take the pup outside, feed him his lunch and then take him out again about ten or so minutes after he's eaten. Also make arrangements with that or another person to be your "emergency" contact if you have to stay late on the job. Remind yourself—repeatedly—that this hectic schedule improves as the puppy gets older.

HOME WITHIN A HOME

Your Chow puppy needs to be confined to one secure, puppy-proof area when no one is able to watch his every move. Generally the kitchen is the place of choice because the floor is washable.

It's hard to distract any dog when he's found something to investigate, but your Chow should learn to always respond to the sound of your voice and to give you his attention.

from first thing in the morning until his bedtime! That's a total of ten or more trips per day to teach the puppy where it's okay to relieve himself. With that schedule in mind, you can see that house-training a young puppy is not a part-time job. It requires someone to be home all day.

EXTRA! EXTRA!
The headlines read: "Puppy Piddles Here!" Breeders commonly use newspapers to line their whelping pens, so puppies learn to associate newspapers with relieving themselves. Do not use newspapers to line your pup's crate, as this will signal to your puppy that it is OK to urinate in his crate. If you choose to paper-train your puppy, you will layer newspapers on a section of the floor near the door he uses to go outside. You should encourage the puppy to use the papers to relieve himself, and bring him there whenever you see him getting ready to go. Little by little, you will reduce the size of the newspaper-covered area so that the puppy will learn to relieve himself "on the other side of the door."

Likewise, it's a busy family area that will accustom the pup to a variety of noises, everything from pots and pans to the telephone, blender and dishwasher. He will also be enchanted by the smell of your cooking (and will never be critical when you burn something). An exercise pen (also called an "ex-pen," a puppy version of a playpen) within the room of choice is an excellent means of confinement for a young pup. He can see out and has a certain amount of space in which to run about, but he is safe from dangerous things like electrical cords, heating units, trash baskets or open kitchen-supply cabinets. Place the pen where the puppy will not get a blast of heat or air conditioning.

In the pen, you can put a few toys, his bed (which can be his crate if the dimensions of pen and crate are compatible) and a few layers of newspaper in one small corner, just in case. A water bowl can be hung at a convenient height on the side of the ex-pen so it won't become a splashing pool for an innovative puppy. His food dish can go on the floor, near but not under the water bowl.

Crates are something that pet owners are at last getting used to for their dogs. Wild or domestic canines have always preferred to sleep in den-like safe spots, and that is exactly what the crate provides. How often have you seen adult dogs that choose to sleep under a table or chair even though they have full run of the house? It's the den connection.

In your "happy" voice, use the word "Crate" every time you put the pup into his den. If he's new to a crate, toss in a small biscuit for him to chase the first few times. At night, after he's been outside, he should sleep in his crate. The crate may be kept in his designated area at night or, if you want to be sure to hear those wake-up yips in the morning, put the crate in a corner of your bedroom. However, don't make any response whatsoever to whining or crying. If he's completely ignored, he'll settle down and get to sleep.

Good bedding for a young puppy is an old folded bath towel or an old blanket, something that is easily washable and disposable if necessary ("accidents" will happen!). Never put newspaper in the puppy's crate. Also those old ideas about adding a clock to replace his mother's heartbeat, or a hot-water bottle to replace her warmth, are just that—old ideas. The clock could drive the puppy nuts, and the hot-water bottle could end up as a very soggy

waterbed! An extremely good breeder would have introduced your puppy to the crate by letting two pups sleep together for a couple of nights, followed by several nights alone. How thankful you will be if you found that breeder!

Safe toys in the pup's crate or area will keep him occupied, but monitor their condition closely. Discard any toys that show signs of being chewed to bits. Squeaky parts, bits of stuffing or plastic or any other small pieces can cause intestinal blockage or possibly choking if swallowed.

Using appropriate food treats as rewards for good performance by your Chow puppy is very helpful as part of your training technique.

TRAINING WITHOUT FOOD

Some dogs (not many!) will respond easily to training if you just smile at them, adding an occasional "Good dog." Positive reinforcement based on praise can replace treats only if done correctly. All correct responses are verbally praised, with the odd pat on the dog's side. Incorrect responses are ignored and the exercise repeated.

PROGRESSING WITH POTTY-TRAINING
After you've taken your puppy out and he has relieved himself in the area you've selected, he can have some free time with the family as long as there is someone responsible for watching him.

The crate has to be your Chow's home within a home. Crates have many useful functions and can be used both indoors and out.

That doesn't mean just someone in the same room who is watching TV or busy on the computer, but one person who is doing nothing other than keeping an eye on the pup, playing with him on the floor and helping him understand his position in the pack.

This first taste of freedom will let you begin to set the house rules. If you don't want the dog on the furniture, now is the time to prevent his first attempts to jump up onto the couch. The word to use in this case is "Off," not "Down." "Down" is the word you will use to teach the down position, which is something entirely different.

Most corrections at this stage come in the form of simply distracting the puppy. Instead of telling him "No" for "Don't chew the carpet," distract the chomping puppy with a toy and he'll forget about the carpet.

A wire crate is preferred for outdoor use, as it allows air to flow through freely. The crate pictured is a good size for the Chow; it should be no smaller.

As you are playing with the pup, do not forget to watch him closely and pay attention to his body language. Whenever you see him begin to circle or sniff, take the puppy outside to relieve himself. If you are paper-training, put him back into his confined area on the newspapers. In either case, praise him as he eliminates while he actually is in the act of relieving himself. Three seconds after he has finished is too late! You'll be praising him for running toward you, or picking up a toy or whatever he may be doing at that moment, and that's not what you want to be praising him for. Timing is a vital tool in all dog training. Use it.

Remove soiled newspapers immediately and replace them with clean ones. You may want to take a small piece of soiled paper

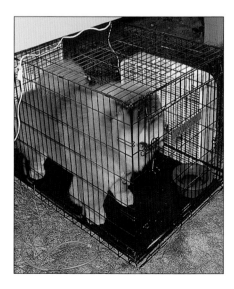

and place it in the middle of the new clean papers, as the scent will attract him to that spot when it's time to go again. That scent attraction is why it's so important to clean up any messes made in the house by using a product specially made to eliminate the odor of dog urine and droppings. Regular household cleansers won't do the trick. Pet shops sell the best pet deodorizers. Invest in the largest container you can find.

Scent attraction eventually will lead your pup to his chosen

Properly trained, a puppy won't resent his leash. In fact, he'll associate it with good things, such as outdoor walks with his beloved master.

LEASH TRAINING

House-training and leash training go hand in hand, literally. When taking your puppy outside to do his business, lead him there on his leash. Unless an emergency potty run is called for, do not whisk the puppy up into your arms and take him outside. If you have a fenced yard, you have the advantage of letting the puppy loose to go out, but it's better to put the dog on the leash and take him to his designated place in the yard until he is reliably house-trained. Taking the puppy for a walk is the best way to house-train a dog. The dog will associate the walk with his time to relieve himself, and the exercise of walking stimulates the dog's bowels and bladder. Dogs that are not trained to relieve themselves on a walk may hold it until they get back home, which of course defeats half the purpose of the walk.

spot outdoors; this is the basis of outdoor training. When you take your puppy outside to relieve himself, use a one-word command such as "Outside" or "Go-potty" (that's one word to the puppy!) as you pick him up and attach his leash. Then put him down in his area. When you know it's time "to go," snap the leash on quickly and lead him to his spot. Now comes the hard part—hard for you, that is. Just stand there until he urinates and defecates. Move him a few feet in one direction or another if he's just sitting there looking at you, but remember that this is neither playtime nor time for a walk. This is strictly a business trip! Then, as he circles and squats (remember your timing!), give him a quiet "Good dog" as

Make sure that your dog's attention is focused on you during training sessons.

a stern voice and get the pup outdoors immediately. No punishment is needed. You and your puppy are just learning each other's language, and sometimes it's easy to miss a puppy's message. Chalk it up to experience and watch more closely from now on.

KEEPING THE PACK ORDERLY

Discipline is a form of training that brings order to life. For example, military discipline is what allows the soldiers in an army to work as one. Discipline is a form of teaching and, in dogs, is the basis of how the successful pack operates. Each member knows his place in the pack and all respect the leader, or Alpha dog. It is essential for your puppy that you establish this type of relationship, with you as the Alpha, or leader. It is a form of social coexistence that all canines recognize and accept. Discipline, therefore, is never to be confused with punishment. When you teach your puppy how you want him to behave, and he behaves properly and you praise him for it, you are disciplining him with a form of positive reinforcement.

For a dog, rewards come in the form of praise, a smile, a cheerful tone of voice, a few friendly pats or a rub of the ears. Rewards are also small food treats. Obviously, that does not mean bits of regular dog food.

praise. If you start to jump for joy, ecstatic over his performance, he'll do one of two things: either he will stop mid-stream, as it were, or he'll do it again for you—in the house—and expect you to be just as delighted!

Give him five minutes or so and, if he doesn't go in that time, take him back indoors to his confined area and try again in another ten minutes, or immediately if you see him sniffing and circling. By careful observation, you'll soon work out a successful schedule.

Accidents, by the way, are just that—accidents. Clean them up quickly and thoroughly, without comment, after the puppy has been taken outside to finish his business and then put back into his area or crate. If you witness an accident in progress, say "No!" in

Instead, treats are very small bits of special things like cheese or pieces of soft dog treats. The idea is to reward the dog with something very small that he can taste and swallow, providing instant positive reinforcement. If he has to take time to chew the treat, by the time he is finished he will have forgotten what he did to earn it!

Your puppy should never be physically punished. The displeasure shown on your face and in your voice is sufficient to signal to the pup that he has done something wrong. He wants to please everyone higher up on the social ladder, especially his leader, so a scowl and harsh voice will take care of the error. Growling out the

SMILE WHEN YOU ORDER ME AROUND!

While trainers recommend practicing with your dog every day, it's perfectly acceptable to take a "mental health day" off. It's better not to train the dog on days when you're in a sour mood. Your bad attitude or lack of interest will be sensed by your dog, and he will respond accordingly. Studies show that dogs are well tuned in to their humans' emotions. Be conscious of how you use your voice when talking to your dog. Raising your voice or shouting will only erode your dog's trust in you as his trainer and master.

word "Shame!" when the pup is caught in the act of doing something wrong is better than the repetitive "No." Some dogs hear "No" so often that they begin to think it's their name! By the way, do not use the dog's name when you're correcting him. His name is reserved to get his attention for something pleasant about to take place.

There are punishments that have nothing to do with you. For example, your dog may think that chasing cats is one reason for his existence. You can try to stop it as much as you like but without success, because it's such fun for the dog. But one good hissing, spitting, swipe of a cat's claws across the dog's nose will put an

Tasty treats or your Chow's favorite toy can be incorporated into your training regimen.

end to the game forever. Intervene only when your dog's eyeball is seriously at risk. Cat scratches can cause permanent damage to an innocent but annoying puppy.

PUPPY KINDERGARTEN

COLLAR AND LEASH

Before you begin your Chow puppy's education, he must be used to his collar and leash. Choose a collar for your puppy that is secure, but not heavy or bulky. He won't enjoy training if he's uncomfortable. A flat buckle collar is fine for everyday wear and for initial puppy training. For

The collar and leash chosen for your puppy's first lessons should be light in weight.

FEAR AGGRESSION

Of the several types of aggression, the one brought on by fear is the most difficult for people to comprehend and to deal with. Aggression to protect food, or any object the dog perceives as his, is more easily understood. Fear aggression is quite different. The dog shows fear, generally for no apparent reason. He backs off, cowers or hides under the bed. If he's on lead, he will hide behind your leg and lash out unexpectedly. No matter how you approach him, he will bite. A fear-biter attacks with great speed and instantly retreats. Don't shout at him or go near him. Don't coddle, sympathize or try to protect him. To him, that's a reward. As with other forms of aggression, get professional help.

---

older dogs, there are several types of training collars such as the martingale, which is a double loop that tightens slightly around the neck, or the head collar, which is similar to a horse's halter. Do not use a chain choke collar unless you have been specifically shown how to put it on and how to use it. You may not be disposed to use a chain choke collar even if your breeder has told you that it's suitable for your Chow.

A lightweight 6-foot woven cotton or nylon training leash is preferred by most trainers because it is easy to fold up in your hand and comfortable to hold because there is a certain amount of give to it. There are lessons where the dog will start off 6 feet away from you at the end of the leash. The leash used to take the puppy outside to relieve himself is shorter because you don't want him to roam away from his area. The shorter leash will also be the one to use when you walk the puppy.

If you've been fortunate enough to enroll in a Puppy Kindergarten Training class, suggestions will be made as to the best collar and leash for your young puppy. I say "fortunate" because your puppy will be in a class with puppies in his age range (up to five months old) of all breeds and sizes. It's the perfect way for him to learn the right way (and the wrong way) to interact with other dogs as well as their people. You cannot teach your puppy how to interpret another dog's sign language. For a first-time puppy owner, these socialization classes are invaluable. For experienced dog owners, they are a real boon to further training.

ATTENTION

You've been using the dog's name since the minute you collected him from the breeder, so you should be able to get his attention by saying his name—with a big smile and in an excited tone of voice. His response will be the puppy equivalent of "Here I am! What are we going to do?" Your immediate response (if you haven't guessed by now) is "Good dog." Rewarding him at the moment he pays attention to you teaches him the proper way to respond when he hears his name.

Puppy or adult, your Chow is definitely intelligent enough to be able to comprehend your instructions. He may be stubborn, but he's smart.

EXERCISES FOR A BASIC CANINE EDUCATION

THE SIT EXERCISE

There are several ways to teach the puppy to sit. The first one is to catch him whenever he is about to sit and, as his backside nears

the floor, say "Sit, good dog!"
That's positive reinforcement and,
if your timing is sharp, he will
learn that what he's doing at that
second is connected to your
saying "Sit" and that you think
he's clever for doing it!

Another method is to start
with the puppy on his leash in
front of you. Show him a treat in
the palm of your right hand. Bring
your hand up under his nose and,
almost in slow motion, move your
hand up and back so his nose
goes up in the air and his head
tilts back as he follows the treat in
your hand. At that point, he will
have to either sit or fall over, so as
his back legs buckle under, say
"Sit, good dog," and then give
him the treat and lots of praise.
You may have to begin with your
hand lightly running up his chest,
actually lifting his chin up until
he sits. Some (usually older) dogs
require gentle pressure on their
hindquarters with the left hand,
in which case the dog should be
on your left side. Puppies generally do not appreciate this physical dominance.

After a few times, you should
be able to show the dog a treat in
the open palm of your hand, raise
your hand waist-high as you say
"Sit" and have him sit. You will
have taught him two things at the
same time, as both the verbal
command and the motion of the
hand are signals for the sit. Your
puppy is watching you almost

RIGHT CLICK ON YOUR DOG

With three clicks, the dolphin jumps
through the hoop. Wouldn't it be nice
to have a dog who could obey
wordless commands that easily?
Clicker training actually was
developed by dolphin trainers and
today is used on dogs with great
success. You can buy a clicker at a pet
shop or pet-supply outlet, and then
you'll be off and clicking.

You can click your dog into
learning new commands, shaping or
conditioning his behavior and solving
bad habits. The clicker, used in
conjunction with a treat, is an
extension of positive reinforcement.
The dog begins to recognize your
happy clicking, and you will never
have to use physical force again. The
dog is conditioned to follow your
hand with the clicker, just as he would
follow your hand with a treat. To
discourage the dog from
inappropriate behavior (like jumping
up or barking), you can use the clicker
to set a timeframe and then click and
reward the dog once he's waited the
allotted time without jumping up or
barking.

more than he is listening to you,
so what you do is just as important as what you say.

Don't save any of these drills
only for training sessions. Use
them as much as possible at odd
times during a normal day. The
dog should always sit before being

given his food dish. He should sit to let you go through a doorway first, when the doorbell rings or when you stop to speak to someone on the street.

THE DOWN EXERCISE

Before beginning to teach the down command, you must consider how the dog feels about this exercise. To him, "down" is a submissive position. Being flat on the floor with you standing over him is not his idea of fun. It's up to you to let him know that, while it may not be fun, the reward of your approval is worth his effort.

Start with the puppy on your left side in a sit position. Hold the leash right above his collar in your left hand. Have an extra-special treat, such as a small piece of cooked chicken or hot dog, in your right hand. Place it at the

GOOD DOWN

"Down" is a harsh-sounding word and a submissive posture in dog body language, thus presenting two obstacles in teaching the down command. When the dog is about to flop down on his own, tell him "Good down." Pups that are not good about being handled learn better by having food lowered in front of them. A dog that trusts you can be gently guided into position. When you give the command "Down," be sure to say it sweetly!

end of the pup's nose and steadily move your hand down and forward along the ground. Hold the leash to prevent a sudden lunge for the food. As the puppy goes into the down position, say "Down" very gently.

The difficulty with this exercise is twofold: it's both the submissive aspect and the fact that most people say the word "Down" as if they were a drill

Once your dog has learned to sit, you can teach him the sit/stay rather easily. Of course, it doesn't hurt to use a treat for extra motivation!

Training the young Chow to stay while off lead is the natural progression from on-lead stay training.

release). Practice this one in the house at various times throughout the day.

By increasing the length of time during which the dog must maintain the down position, you'll find many uses for it. For example, he can lie at your feet in the vet's office or anywhere that both of you have to wait, when you are on the phone, while the family is eating and so forth. If you progress to training for competitive obedience, he'll already be all set for the exercise called the "long down."

THE STAY EXERCISE

You can teach your Chow to stay in the sit, down and stand positions. To teach the sit/stay, have the dog sit on your left side. Hold the leash at waist level in your left hand and let the dog know that you have a treat in your

sergeant in charge of recruits! So issue the command sweetly, give him the treat and have the pup maintain the down position for several seconds. If he tries to get up immediately, place your hands on his shoulders and press down gently, giving him a very quiet "Good dog." As you progress with this lesson, increase the "down time" until he will hold it until you say "Okay" (his cue for

BOOT CAMP

Even if one member of the family assumes the role of "drill sergeant," every other member of the family has to know what's involved in the dog's education. Success depends on consistency and knowing what words to use, how to use them, how to say them, when to say them and, most important to the dog, how to praise. The dog will be happy to respond to all members of the family, but don't make the little guy think he's in boot camp!

closed right hand. Step forward on your right foot as you say "Stay." Immediately turn and stand directly in front of the dog, keeping your right hand up high so he'll keep his eye on the treat hand and maintain the sit position for a count of five. Return to your original position and offer the reward.

Increase the length of the sit/stay each time until the dog can hold it for at least 30 seconds without moving. After about a week of success, move out on your right foot and take two steps before turning to face the dog. Give the "Stay" hand signal (left palm back toward the dog's head) as you leave. He gets the treat when you return and he holds the sit/stay. Increase the distance that you walk away from him before turning until you reach the length of your training leash. But don't rush it! Go back to the beginning if he moves before he should. No matter what the lesson, never be upset by having to back up for a few days. The repetition and practice are what will make your dog reliable in these commands. It won't do any good to move on to something more difficult if the command is not mastered at the easier levels. Above all, even if you do get frustrated, never let your puppy know! Always keep a positive, upbeat attitude during training, which will transmit to your dog for positive results.

The down/stay is taught in the same way once the dog is completely reliable and steady with the down command. Again, don't rush it. With the dog in the down position on your left side, step out on your right foot as you say "Stay." Return by walking around in back of the dog and into your original position. While you are training, it's okay to murmur something like "Hold on" to encourage him to stay put. When the dog will stay without moving when you are at a distance of 3 or 4 feet, begin to increase the length of time before you return. Be sure he holds the down on your return until you say "Okay." At that point, he gets his

It feels good to be able to reward your Chow for a fine performance during a training session.

COME AND GET IT!

The come command is your dog's safety signal. Until he is 99% perfect in responding, don't use the come command if you cannot enforce it. Practice on leash with treats or squeakers, or whenever the dog is running to you. Never call him to come to you if he is to be corrected for a misdemeanor. Reward the dog with a treat and happy praise whenever he comes to you.

treat—just so he'll remember for next time that it's not over until it's over.

THE COME EXERCISE

No command is more important to the safety of your Chow than "Come." It is what you should say every single time you see the puppy running toward you: "Rebel, come! Good dog." During playtime, run a few feet away from the puppy and turn and tell him to "Come" as he is already running to you. You can go so far

as to teach your puppy two things at once if you squat down and hold out your arms. As the pup gets close to you and you're saying "Good dog," bring your right arm in about waist high. Now he's also learning the hand signal, an excellent device should you be on the phone when you need to get him to come to you! You'll also both be one step ahead when you enter obedience classes.

Puppies, like children, have notoriously short attention spans, so don't overdo it with any of the training. Keep each lesson short. Break it up with a quick run around the yard or a ball toss, repeat the lesson and quit as soon as the pup gets it right. That way, you will always end with a "Good dog."

When the puppy responds to your well-timed "Come," try it with the puppy on the training leash. This time, catch him off guard, while he's sniffing a leaf or watching a bird: "Rebel, come!" You may have to pause for a split second after his name to be sure you have his attention. If the puppy shows any sign of confusion, give the leash a mild jerk and take a couple of steps backward. Do not repeat the command. In this case, you should say "Good come" as he reaches you.

That's the number-one rule of training. Each command word is given just once. Anything more is nagging. You'll also notice that all commands are one word only. Even when they are actually two words, you say them as one.

Never call the dog to come to you—with or without his name—if you are angry or intend to correct him for some misbehavior. When correcting the pup, you go to him. Your dog must always connect "come" with something pleasant and with your approval; then you can rely on his response.

Life isn't perfect and neither are puppies. A time will come, often around 10 months of age, when he'll become "selectively deaf" or choose to "forget" his name. He may respond by wagging his tail (and even seeming to smile at you) with a look that says "Make me!" Laugh, throw his favorite toy and skip the lesson you had planned. Pups will be pups!

THE HEEL EXERCISE

The second most important command to teach, after the come, is the heel. When you are walking your growing puppy, you need to be in control. Besides, it looks terrible to be pulled and yanked down the street, and it's not much fun either. Your eight-to ten-week-old puppy will probably follow you everywhere, but that's his natural instinct, not your control over the situation. However, any time he does follow you, you can say "Heel" and be ahead of the

If your Chow learns as a pup to associate coming to you with treats and praise, he will think of it as a positive experience and should never fail to come when called.

game, as he will learn to associate this command with the action of following you before you even begin teaching him to heel.

There is a very precise, almost military, procedure for teaching your dog to heel. As with all other obedience training, begin with the dog on your left side. He will be in a very nice sit and you will have the training leash across your chest. Hold the loop and folded leash in your right hand. Pick up the slack leash above the dog in your left hand and hold it loosely at your side. Step out on your left foot as you say "Heel." If the puppy does not move, give a gentle tug or pat your left leg to get him started. If he surges ahead of you, stop and pull him back

TAPERING OFF TIDBITS

Your dog has been watching you—and the hand that treats—throughout all of his lessons, and now it's time to break the treat habit. Begin by giving him treats at the end of each lesson only. Then start to give a treat after the end of only some of the lessons. At the end of every lesson, as well as during the lessons, be consistent with the praise. Your pup now doesn't know whether he'll get a treat or not, but he should keep performing well just in case! Finally, you will stop giving treat rewards entirely. Save them for something brand-new that you want to teach him. Keep up the praise and you'll always have a "good dog."

gently until he is at your side. Tell him to sit and begin again.

Walk a few steps and stop while the puppy is correctly beside you. Tell him to sit and give mild verbal praise. (More enthusiastic praise will encourage him to think the lesson is over.) Repeat the lesson, increasing the number of steps you take only as long as the dog is heeling nicely beside you. When you end the lesson, have him hold the sit, then give him the "Okay" to let him know that this is the end of the lesson. Praise him so that he knows he did a good job.

The cure for excessive pulling (a common problem) is to stop when the dog is no more than 2 or 3 feet ahead of you. Guide him back into position and begin again. With a really determined puller, try switching to a head collar. This will automatically turn the pup's head toward you so you can bring him back easily to the heel position. Give quiet, reassuring praise every time the leash goes slack and he's staying with you.

Staying and heeling can take a lot out of a dog, so provide playtime and free-running exercise to shake off the stress when the lessons are over. You don't want him to associate training with all work and no fun.

OBEDIENCE CLASSES

The advantages of an obedience class are that your dog will have to learn amid the distractions of other people and dogs and that your mistakes will be quickly corrected by the trainer. Teaching your dog along with a qualified instructor and other handlers who may have more dog experience than you is another plus of the class environment. The instructor and other handlers can help you to find the most efficient way of teaching your dog a command or exercise. It's often easier to learn by other people's mistakes than your own. You will also learn all of the requirements for competitive obedience trials, in which you can earn titles and go on to advanced jumping and retrieving exercises, which are fun for many dogs. Obedience classes build the foundation needed for many other canine activities (in which we humans are allowed to participate, too!).

TRAINING FOR OTHER ACTIVITIES

Once your dog has basic obedience under his collar and is 12 months of age, you can enter the world of agility training. Dogs think agility is pure fun, like being turned loose in an amusement park full of obstacles! In addition to agility, there are hunting activities for sporting dogs, lure-coursing events for sighthounds, go-to-ground events for terriers, racing for the Nordic sled dogs, herding trials for the

shepherd breeds and tracking, which is open to all "nosey" dogs (which would include all dogs!). For those who like to volunteer, there is the wonderful feeling of owning a therapy dog and visiting hospices, nursing homes and veterans' homes to bring smiles, comfort and companionship to those who live there.

Around the house, your Chow can be taught to do some simple chores. You might teach him to carry a basket of household items or to fetch the morning newspaper. The kids can teach the dog all kinds of tricks, from playing hide-and-seek to balancing a biscuit on his nose. A family dog is what rounds out the family. Everything he does beyond sitting in your lap or gazing lovingly at you represents the bonus of owning a dog.

Who are you calling "non-sporting"? Here's an aquatic Chow getting some daily exercise!

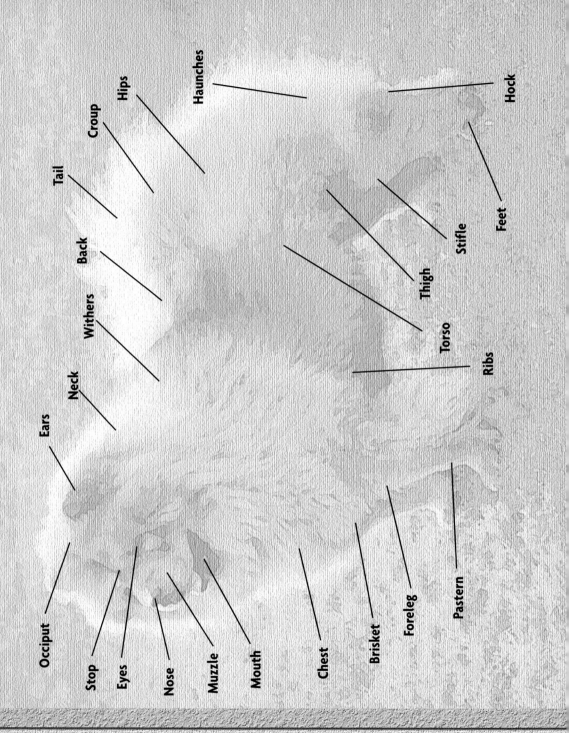

Haunches

Hips

Croup

Tail

Back

Withers

Neck

Ears

Occiput

Stop

Eyes

Nose

Muzzle

Mouth

Chest

Brisket

Foreleg

Pastern

Ribs

Torso

Thigh

Stifle

Feet

Hock

PHYSICAL STRUCTURE OF THE CHOW CHOW

HEALTHCARE OF YOUR

CHOW CHOW

By Lowell Ackerman DVM, DACVD

HEALTHCARE FOR A LIFETIME

When you own a dog, you become his healthcare advocate over his entire lifespan, as well as being the one to shoulder the financial burden of such care. Accordingly, it is worthwhile to focus on prevention rather than treatment, as you and your pet will both be happier.

Of course, the best place to have begun your program of preventive healthcare is with the initial purchase or adoption of your dog. There is no way of guaranteeing that your new furry friend is free of medical problems, but there are some things you can do to improve your odds. You certainly should have done adequate research into the Chow and have selected your puppy carefully rather than buying on impulse. Health issues aside, a large number of pet abandonment and relinquishment cases arise from a mismatch between pet needs and owner expectations. This is entirely preventable with appropriate planning and finding a good breeder.

Regarding healthcare issues specifically, it is very difficult to make blanket statements about where to acquire a problem-free pet, but, again, a reputable breeder is your best bet. In an ideal situation you have the opportunity to see both parents, get references from other owners of the breeder's pups and see genetic-testing documentation for several generations of the litter's ancestors. At the very least, you must thoroughly investigate your breed of interest and the problems inherent in that breed, as well as the genetic testing available to screen for those problems. Genetic testing offers some important benefits, but testing is available for only a few disorders in a relatively small number of breeds and is not available for some of the most common genetic diseases, such as hip dysplasia, cataracts, epilepsy, cardiomyopathy, etc. This area of research is indeed exciting and increasingly important, and advances will continue to be made each year. In fact, recent research has shown that there is an equivalent dog gene for

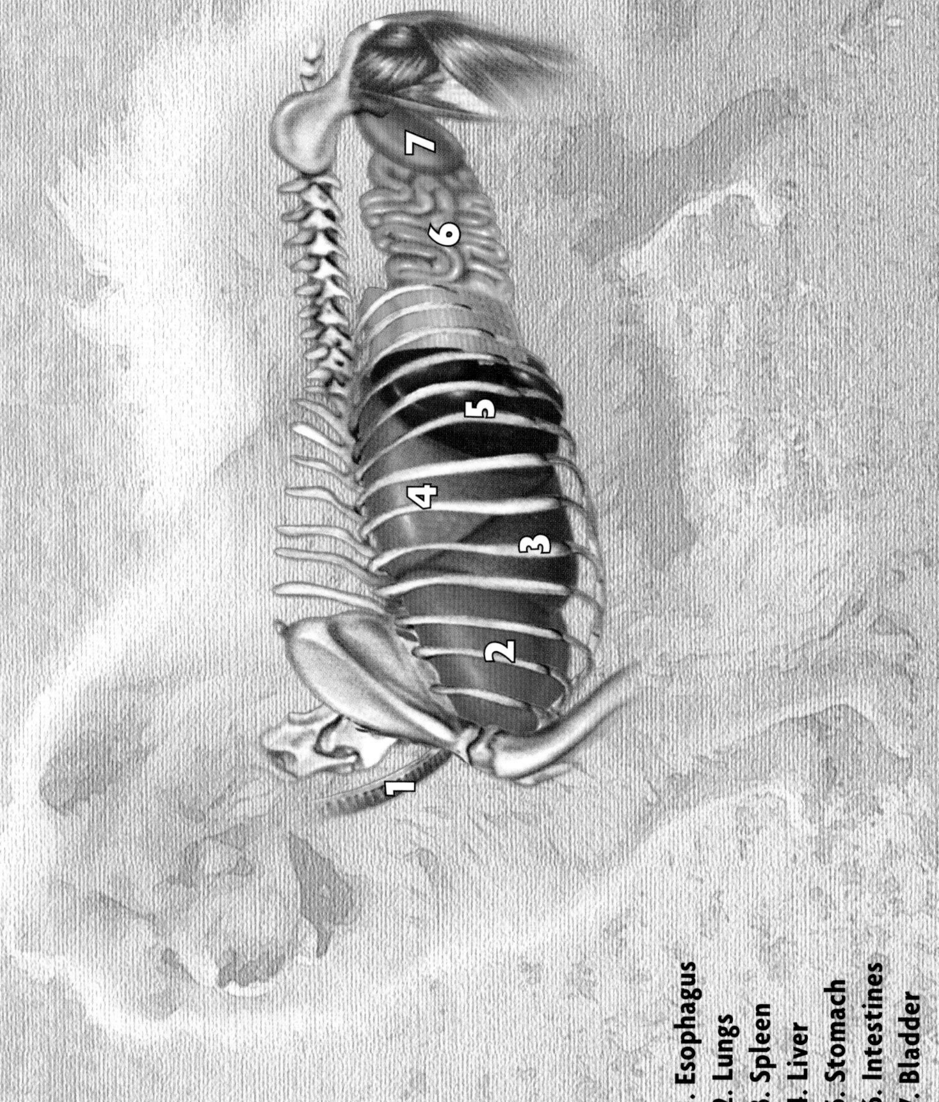

1. Esophagus
2. Lungs
3. Spleen
4. Liver
5. Stomach
6. Intestines
7. Bladder

Internal Organs of the Chow Chow

75% of known human genes, so research done in either species is likely to benefit the other.

We've also discussed that evaluating the behavioral nature of your Chow and that of his immediate family members is an important part of the selection process that cannot be underestimated or overemphasized. It is sometimes difficult to evaluate temperament in puppies because certain behavioral tendencies, such as some forms of aggression, may not be immediately evident. More dogs are euthanized each year for behavioral reasons than for all medical conditions combined, so it is critical to take temperament issues seriously. Start with a well-balanced, friendly companion and put the time and effort into proper socialization, and you will both be rewarded with a lifelong valued relationship.

Assuming that you have started off with a pup from healthy, sound stock, you then become responsible for helping your veterinarian keep your pet healthy. Some crucial things happen before you even bring your puppy home. Parasite control typically begins at two weeks of age, and vaccinations typically begin at six to eight weeks of age. A pre-pubertal evaluation is typically scheduled for about six months of age. At this time, a dental evaluation is done

(since the adult teeth are now in), heartworm prevention is started and neutering or spaying is most commonly done.

It is critical to commence regular dental care at home if you have not already done so. It may not sound very important, but most dogs have active periodontal disease by four years of age if they don't have their teeth cleaned regularly at home, not just at their veterinary exams. Dental problems lead to more than just bad "doggie breath": gum disease can have very serious medical consequences. If you start brushing your dog's teeth and using antiseptic rinses from a young age, your dog will be accustomed to it and will not resist. The results will be healthy dentition, which your pet will need to enjoy a long, healthy life.

Most dogs are considered adults at a year of age, although some larger breeds still have some filling out to do up to about two or so years old. Even individual dogs within each breed have different healthcare requirements, so work with your veterinarian to determine what will be needed and what your role should be. This doctor-client relationship is important, because as vaccination guidelines change, there may not be an annual "vaccine visit" scheduled. You must make sure that you see your veterinarian at least annually, even if no vaccines

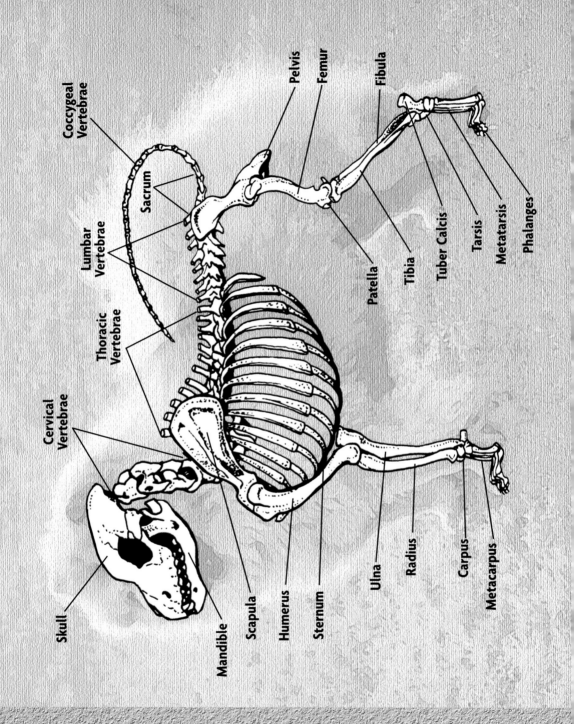

Coccygeal Vertebrae

Pelvis

Femur

Fibula

Sacrum

Lumbar Vertebrae

Thoracic Vertebrae

Patella

Tibia

Tuber Calcis

Tarsis

Metatarsis

Phalanges

Cervical Vertebrae

Ulna

Radius

Carpus

Metacarpus

Skull

Mandible

Scapula

Humerus

Sternum

SKELETAL STRUCTURE OF THE CHOW CHOW

are due, because this is the best opportunity to coordinate healthcare activities and to make sure that no medical issues creep by unaddressed.

When your Chow reaches three-quarters of his anticipated lifespan, he is considered a "senior" and likely requires some special care. In general, if you've been taking great care of your canine companion throughout his formative and adult years, the transition to senior status should be a smooth one. Age is not a disease, and as long as everything is functioning as it should, there is no reason why most of late adulthood should not be rewarding for both you and your pet. This is especially true if you have tended to the details, such as regular veterinary visits, proper dental care, excellent nutrition and management of bone and joint issues.

At this stage in your Chow's life, your veterinarian may want to schedule visits twice yearly, instead of once, to run some laboratory screenings, electrocardiograms and the like, and to change the diet to something more digestible. Catching problems early is the best way to manage them effectively. Treating the early stages of heart disease is so much easier than trying to intervene when there is more significant damage to the heart muscle. Similarly, managing the beginning of

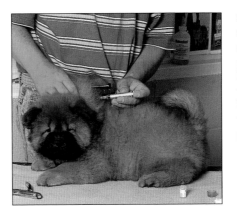

One of the first things you should do with your Chow puppy is to bring him to a local veterinarian and have him examined for health problems.

kidney problems is fairly routine if there is no significant kidney damage. Other problems, like cognitive dysfunction (similar to senility and Alzheimer's disease), cancer, diabetes and arthritis, are more common in older dogs, but all can be treated to help the dog live as many happy, comfortable years as possible. Just as in people, medical management is more effective (and less expensive) when you catch things early.

SELECTING A VETERINARIAN
There is probably no more important decision that you will make regarding your pet's healthcare than the selection of his doctor. Your pet's veterinarian will be a pediatrician, family-practice physician and gerontologist, depending on the dog's life stage, and will be the individual who makes recommendations regarding issues such as when specialists need to be consulted, when diagnostic testing and/or thera-

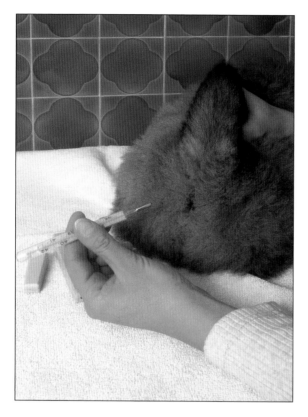

You should learn how to take your Chow's temperature at home.

pets. For others, they are seeking a clinician with keen diagnostic and therapeutic insight who can deliver state-of-the-art healthcare. Still others need a veterinary facility that is open evenings and weekends, or is in close proximity or provides mobile veterinary services, to accommodate their schedules; these people may not much mind that their dogs might see different veterinarians on each visit. Just as we have different

peutic intervention is needed and when you will need to seek outside emergency and critical-care services. Your vet will act as your advocate and liaison throughout these processes.

Everyone has his own idea about what to look for in a vet, an individual who will play a big role in his dog's (and, of course, his own) life for many years to come. For some, it is the compassionate caregiver with whom they hope to develop a professional relationship to span the lifetime of their dogs and even their future

TAKING YOUR DOG'S TEMPERATURE

It is important to know how to take your dog's temperature at times when you think he may be ill. It's not the most enjoyable task, but it can be done without too much difficulty. It's easier with a helper, preferably someone with whom the dog is friendly, so that one of you can hold the dog while the other inserts the thermometer.

Before inserting the thermometer, coat the end with petroleum jelly. Insert the thermometer slowly and gently into the dog's rectum about one inch. Wait for the reading, about two minutes. Be sure to remove the thermometer carefully and clean it thoroughly after each use.

A dog's normal body temperature is between 100.5 and 102.5 degrees F. Immediate veterinary attention is required if the dog's temperature is below 99 or above 104 degrees F.

reasons for selecting our own healthcare professionals (e.g., covered by insurance plan, expert in field, convenient location, etc.), we should not expect that there is a one-size-fits-all recommendation for selecting a veterinarian and veterinary practice. The best advice is to be honest in your assessment of what you expect from a veterinary practice and to conscientiously research the options in your area. You will quickly appreciate that not all veterinary practices are the same, and you will be happiest with one that truly meets your needs.

There is another point to be considered in the selection of veterinary services. Not that long ago, a single veterinarian would attempt to manage all medical and surgical issues as they arose. That was often problematic, because veterinarians are trained in many species and many diseases, and it was just impossible for general veterinary practitioners to be experts in every species, every field and every ailment. However, just as in the human healthcare fields, specialization has allowed general practitioners to concentrate on primary healthcare delivery, especially wellness and the prevention of infectious diseases, and to utilize a network of specialists to assist in the management of conditions that require specific expertise and experience. Thus there are now many types of

veterinary specialists, including dermatologists, cardiologists, ophthalmologists, surgeons, internists, oncologists, neurologists, behaviorists, criticalists and others to help primary-care veterinarians deal with complicated medical challenges. In most cases, specialists see cases referred by primary-care veterinarians, make diagnoses and set up management plans. From there, the animals' ongoing care is returned to their primary-care veterinarians. This important team approach to your pet's medical-care needs has provided opportunities for advanced care and an unparalleled level of quality to be delivered.

With all of the opportunities for your Chow to receive high-quality veterinary medical care, there is another topic that needs to be addressed at the same time—cost. It's been said that you can have excellent healthcare or inexpensive healthcare, but never both; this is as true in veterinary medicine as it is in human medicine. While veterinary costs are a fraction of what the same services cost in the human healthcare arena, it is still difficult to deal with unanticipated medical costs, especially since they can easily creep into hundreds or even thousands of dollars if specialists or emergency services become involved. However, there are ways of managing these risks. The easiest is to buy pet health insurance and realize that its foremost purpose is not to cover routine healthcare visits but rather to serve as an umbrella for those rainy days when your pet needs medical care and you don't want to worry about whether or not you can afford that care.

Pet insurance policies are very cost-effective (and very inexpensive by human health-insurance standards), but make sure that you buy the policy long before you intend to use it (preferably starting in puppyhood, because coverage will exclude pre-existing conditions) and that you are actually buying an indemnity insurance plan from an insurance company that is regulated by your state or province. Many insurance policy look-alikes are actually discount clubs that are redeemable only at specific locations and for specific services. An indemnity plan covers your pet at almost all veterinary, specialty and emergency practices and is an excellent way to manage your pet's ongoing healthcare needs.

VACCINATIONS AND INFECTIOUS DISEASES

There has never been an easier time to prevent a variety of infectious diseases in your dog, but the advances we've made in veteri-

SAMPLE VACCINATION SCHEDULE

6–8 weeks of age	Parvovirus, Distemper, Adenovirus-2 (Hepatitis)
9–11 weeks of age	Parvovirus, Distemper, Adenovirus-2 (Hepatitis)
12–14 weeks of age	Parvovirus, Distemper, Adenovirus-2 (Hepatitis)
16–20 weeks of age	Rabies
1 year of age	Parvovirus, Distemper, Adenovirus-2 (Hepatitis), Rabies

Revaccination is performed every one to three years, depending on the product, the method of administration and the patient's risk. Initial adult inoculation (for dogs at least 16 weeks of age in which a puppy series was not done or could not be confirmed) is two vaccinations, done three to four weeks apart, with revaccination according to the same criteria mentioned. Other vaccines are given as decided between owner and veterinarian.

nary medicine come with a price—choice. Now while it may seem that choice is a good thing (and it is), it has never been more difficult for the pet owner (or the veterinarian) to make an informed decision about the best way to protect pets through vaccination.

Years ago, it was just accepted that puppies got a starter series of vaccinations and then annual "boosters" throughout their lives to keep them protected. As more and more vaccines became available, consumers wanted the convenience of having all of that protection in a single injection. The result was "multivalent" vaccines that crammed a lot of protection into a single syringe. The manufacturers' recommendations were to give the vaccines annually, and this was a simple enough protocol to follow. However, as veterinary medicine has become more sophisticated and we have started looking more at healthcare quandaries rather than convenience, it became necessary to reevaluate the situation and deal with some tough questions. It is important to realize that whether or not to use a particular vaccine depends on the risk of contracting the disease against which it protects, the severity of the disease if it is contracted, the duration of immunity provided by the vaccine, the safety of the product and the needs of the individual animal. In

a very general sense, rabies, distemper, hepatitis and parvovirus are considered core vaccine needs, while parainfluenza, *Bordetella bronchiseptica*, leptospirosis, coronavirus and borreliosis (Lyme disease) are considered non-core needs and best reserved for animals that demonstrate reasonable risk of contracting the diseases.

THE GREAT VACCINATION DEBATE
What kinds of questions need to be addressed? When the vet injects multiple organisms at the same time, might some of the components interfere with one another in the development of immunologic protection? We don't have the comprehensive answer for that question, but it does appear that the immune system better handles agents

PUPPY SHOTS
Puppies are born with natural antibodies that protect them from most canine diseases. They receive more antibodies from the colostrum in their mother's milk. These immunities wear off, however, and must be replaced through a series of vaccines. Puppy shots are given at 3- to 4-week intervals starting at 6 to 8 weeks of age through 16 to 20 weeks of age. Booster shots are given after one year of age, and every one to three years thereafter.

COMMON INFECTIOUS DISEASES

Let's discuss some of the diseases that create the need for vaccination in the first place. Following are the major canine infectious diseases and a simple explanation of each.

Rabies: A devastating viral disease that can be fatal in dogs and people. In fact, vaccination of dogs and cats is an important public-health measure to create a resistant animal buffer population to protect people from contracting the disease. Vaccination schedules are determined on a government level and are not optional for pet owners; rabies vaccination is required by law in all 50 states.

Parvovirus: A severe, potentially life-threatening disease that is easily transmitted between dogs. There are four strains of the virus, but it is believed that there is significant "cross-protection" between strains that may be included in individual vaccines.

Distemper: A potentially severe and life-threatening disease with a relatively high risk of exposure, especially in certain regions. In very high-risk distemper environments, young pups may be vaccinated with human measles vaccine, a related virus that offers cross-protection when administered at four to ten weeks of age.

Hepatitis: Caused by canine adenovirus type 1 (CAV-1), but since vaccination with the causative virus has a higher rate of adverse effects, cross-protection is derived from the use of adenovirus type 2 (CAV-2), a cause of respiratory disease and one of the potential causes of canine cough. Vaccination with CAV-2 provides long-term immunity against hepatitis, but relatively less protection against respiratory infection.

Canine cough: Also called tracheobronchitis, actually a fairly complicated result of viral and bacterial offenders; therefore, even with vaccination, protection is incomplete. Wherever dogs congregate, canine cough will likely be spread among them. Intranasal vaccination with *Bordetella* and parainfluenza is the best safeguard, but the duration of immunity does not appear to be very long, typically a year at most. These are non-core vaccines, but vaccination is sometimes mandated by boarding kennels, obedience classes, dog shows and other places where dogs congregate to try to minimize spread of infection.

Leptospirosis: A potentially fatal disease that is more common in some geographic regions. It is capable of being spread to humans. The disease varies with the individual "serovar," or strain, of *Leptospira* involved. Since there does not appear to be much cross-protection between serovars, protection is only as good as the likelihood that the serovar in the vaccine is the same as the one in the pet's local environment. Problems with *Leptospira* vaccines are that protection does not last very long, side effects are not uncommon and a large percentage of dogs (perhaps 30%) may not respond to vaccination.

Borrelia burgdorferi: The cause of Lyme disease, the risk of which varies with the geographic area in which the pet lives and travels. Lyme disease is spread by deer ticks in the eastern US and western black-legged ticks in the western part of the country, and the risk of exposure is high in some regions. Lameness, fever and inappetence are most commonly seen in affected dogs. The extent of protection from the vaccine has not been conclusively demonstrated.

Coronavirus: This disease has a high risk of exposure, especially in areas where dogs congregate, but it typically causes only mild to moderate digestive upset (diarrhea, vomiting, etc.). Vaccines are available, but the duration of protection is believed to be relatively short and the effectiveness of the vaccine in preventing infection is considered low.

There are many other vaccinations available, including those for *Giardia* and canine adenovirus-1. While there may be some specific indications for their use, and local risk factors to be considered, they are not widely recommended for most dogs.

when given individually. Unfortunately, most manufacturers still bundle their vaccine components because that is what most pet owners want, so getting vaccines with single components can sometimes be difficult.

Another question has to do with how often vaccines should be given. Again, this seems to be different for each vaccine component. There seems to be a general consensus that a puppy (or a dog with an unknown vaccination history) should get a series of vaccinations to initially stimulate his immunity and then a booster at one year of age, but even the veterinary associations and colleges have trouble reaching agreement about what he should get after that. Rabies vaccination schedules are not debated, because vaccine schedules for this contagious and devastating disease are determined by government agencies. Regarding the rest, some recommend that we continue to give the vaccines annually because this method has worked well as a disease preventive for decades and delivers predictable protection. Others recommend that some of the vaccines need to be given only every second or third year, as this can be done without affecting levels of protection. This is probably true for some vaccine components (such as hepatitis), but there

have been no large studies to demonstrate what the optimal interval should be and whether the same principles hold true for all breeds.

It may be best to just measure titers, which are protective blood levels of various vaccine components, on an annual basis, but that too is not without controversy. Scientists have not precisely determined the minimum titer of specific vaccine components that will be guaranteed to provide a pet with protection. Pets with very high titers will clearly be protected and those with very low

BEWARE THE SPIDER

Should you worry about having a spider spinning her mucilaginous web over your dog? Like other venomous critters, spiders can bite dogs and cause severe reactions. The most deleterious eight-leggers are the black and red widow spiders, brown recluse and common brown spiders, whose bites can cause local pain, cramping, spasms and restlessness. These signals tell owners there is a problem, as the bites themselves can be difficult to locate under your dog's coat. Another vicious arachnid is the bark scorpion, whose bite can cause excessive drooling, tearing, urination and defecation. Often spider and scorpion bites are misdiagnosed because vets don't recognize the signs and owners didn't witness the escape of the avenging arachnid.

HIT ME WITH A HOT SPOT

What is a hot spot? Technically known as pyotraumatic dermatitis, a hot spot is an infection on the dog's coat, usually by the rear end, under the tail or on a leg, which the dog inflicts upon himself. The dog licks and bites the itchy spot until it becomes inflamed and infected. The hot spot can range in size from the circumference of a grape to the circumference of an apple. Provided that the hot spot is not related to a deeper bacterial infection, it can be treated topically by clipping the area, cleaning the sore and giving prednisone. For bacterial infections, antibiotics are required. In some cases, an Elizabethan collar is required to keep the dog from further irritating the hot spot. The itching can intensify and the pain becomes worse. Medicated shampoos and cool compresses, drying agents and topical steroids may be prescribed by your vet as well.

Hot spots can be caused by fleas, an allergy, an ear infection, anal sac problems, mange or a foreign irritant. Likewise, they can be linked to psychoses. The underlying problem must be addressed in addition to the hot spot itself.

nation, depending on their risk of coming into contact with the disease.

These questions leave primary-care veterinarians in a very uncomfortable position, one that is not easy to resolve. Do they recommend annual vaccination in a manner that has demonstrated successful protection for decades, do they recommend skipping vaccines some years and hope that the protection lasts or do they measure blood tests (titers) and hope that the results are convincing enough to clearly indicate whether repeat vaccination is warranted?

These aren't the only vaccination questions impacting pets, owners and veterinarians. Other controversies focus on whether vaccines should be dosed according to body weight (currently they are administered in uniform doses, regardless of the animal's size), whether there are breed-specific issues important in determining vaccination programs (for instance, we know that some breeds have a harder time mounting an appropriate immune response to parvovirus vaccine and might benefit from a different dose or injection interval) and which type of vaccine—live-virus or inactivated—offers more advantages with fewer disadvantages. Clearly, there are many more questions than there are answers. The important thing, as a pet owner, is to be aware of the issues

titers will need repeat vaccinations, but there is also a large "gray zone" of pets that probably have intermediate protection and may or may not need repeat vacci-

and be able to work with your veterinarian to make decisions that are right for your pet. Be an informed consumer and you will appreciate the deliberation required in tailoring a vaccination program to best meet the needs of your pet. Expect also that this is an ongoing, ever-changing topic of debate; thus, the decisions you

make this year won't necessarily be the same as the ones you make next year.

NEUTERING/SPAYING

Sterilization procedures (neutering for males/spaying for females) are meant to accomplish several purposes. While the underlying premise is to address the risk of pet overpopulation, there are also some medical and behavioral benefits to the surgeries as well. For females, spaying prior to the first estrus (heat cycle) leads to a marked reduction in the risk of mammary cancer. There also will be no manifestations of "heat" to attract male dogs and no bleeding in the house. For males, there is prevention of testicular cancer and a reduction in the risk of prostate problems. In both sexes there may be some limited reduction in aggressive behaviors toward other dogs, and some

Your dog's diet is one of the biggest factors in his degree of good health, with both the type of food and the amount fed of great importance.

PSEUDOPREGNANCY

Your female dog can experience a pseudopregnancy if she is not bred during her estrous cycle. This pseudocyesis usually occurs about eight weeks after her period and is accompanied by swollen mammary glands and an enlarged abdomen. Your bitch may "adopt" one of her toys as her litter and demonstrate nesting behavior (digging a burrow in your couch or her bed). She may also exhibit aggressive behavior toward humans who attempt to threaten her "litter."

Pseudocyesis may trace back to wolf behavior in the wild. Commonly the aunts or granddam of a litter will assist another bitch in the pack with her litter. All of the bitches will feed the pups and protect them.

Since there are health risks involved with pseudopregnancy, owners are advised to spay their bitches to prevent a recurrence. Bitches can suffer from uterine infections, which can threaten their lives.

DOGGIE DENTAL DON'TS

A veterinary dental exam is necessary if you notice one or any combination of the following in your dog:
- Broken, loose or missing teeth
- Loss of appetite (which could be due to mouth pain or illness caused by infection)
- Gum abnormalities, including redness, swelling and bleeding
- Drooling, with or without blood
- Yellowing of the teeth or gumline, indicating tartar
- Bad breath

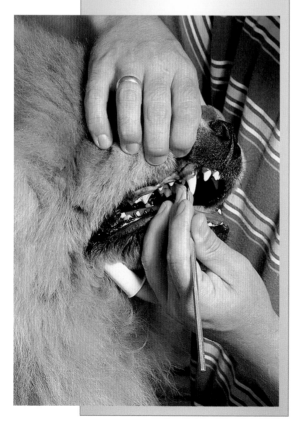

diminishing of urine marking, roaming and mounting.

While neutering and spaying do indeed prevent animals from contributing to pet overpopulation, even no-cost and low-cost neutering options have not eliminated the problem. Perhaps one of the main reasons for this is that individuals who intentionally breed their dogs and those who allow their animals to run at large are the main causes of unwanted offspring. Also, animals in shelters are often there because they were abandoned or relinquished, not because they came from unplanned matings. Neutering/spaying is important, but it should be considered in the context of the real causes of animals' ending up in shelters and eventually being euthanized.

One of the important considerations regarding neutering is that it is a surgical procedure. This sometimes gets lost in discussions of low-cost procedures and commoditization of the process. In females, spaying is specifically referred to as an ovariohysterectomy. In this procedure, a midline incision is made in the abdomen and the entire uterus and both ovaries are surgically removed. While this is a major invasive surgical procedure, it usually has few complications, because it is typically performed on healthy young animals. However, it is major surgery, as any woman who has had a hysterectomy will attest.

In males, neutering has traditionally referred to castration, which involves the surgical removal of both testicles. While still a significant piece of surgery, there is not the abdominal exposure that is required in the female surgery. In addition, there is now a chemical sterilization option, in which a solution is injected into each testicle, leading to atrophy of the sperm-producing cells. This can typically be done under sedation rather than full anesthesia. This is a relatively new approach, and there are no long-term clinical studies yet available.

Neutering/spaying is typically done around six months of age at most veterinary hospitals, although techniques have been pioneered to perform the procedures in animals as young as eight weeks of age. In general, the surgeries on the very young animals are done for the specific reason of sterilizing them before they go to their new homes. This is done in some shelter hospitals for assurance that the animals will definitely not produce any pups. Otherwise, these organizations need to rely on owners to comply with their wishes to have the animals "altered" at a later date, something that does not always happen.

There are some exciting immunocontraceptive "vaccines" currently under development, and

there may be a time when contraception in pets will not require surgical procedures. We anxiously await these developments.

Exercise is important for your dog. Chows, with the possible exception of some very aged dogs, enjoy romping with their owners.

SPAY'S THE WAY

Although spaying a female dog qualifies as major surgery—an ovariohysterectomy, in fact—this procedure is regarded as routine when performed by a qualified veterinarian on a healthy dog. The advantages to spaying a bitch are many and great. Spayed dogs do not develop uterine cancer or any life-threatening diseases of the genitals. Likewise, spayed dogs are at a significantly reduced risk of breast cancer. Bitches (and owners) are relieved of the demands of heat cycles. A spayed bitch will not leave bloody stains on your furniture during estrus, and you will not have to contend with single-minded macho males trying to climb your fence in order to seduce her. The spayed bitch's coat will not show the ill effects of her estrogen level's climbing such as a dull, lackluster outer coat or patches of hairlessness.

EXTERNAL PARASITES

FLEAS

Fleas have been around for millions of years and, while we have better tools now for controlling them than at any time in the past, there still is little chance that they will end up on an endangered species list. Actually, they are very well adapted to living on our pets, and they continue to adapt as we make advances.

The female flea can consume 15 times her weight in blood during active reproduction and can lay as many as 40 eggs a day. These eggs are very resistant to the effects of insecticides. They hatch into larvae, which then mature and spin cocoons. The immature fleas reside in this pupal stage until the time is right for feeding. This pupal stage is also very resistant to the effects of insecticides, and pupae can last in the environment without feeding for many months. Newly emergent fleas are attracted to animals by the warmth of the animals' bodies, movement and exhaled carbon dioxide. However, when they first emerge from their cocoons, they orient towards light; thus when an animal passes between a flea and the light source, casting a shadow, the flea pounces and starts to feed. If the animal turns out to be a dog or cat, the reproductive cycle continues. If the flea lands on another type of animal, including a person, the flea will bite but will then look for a more appropriate host. An emerging adult flea can survive without feeding for up to 12 months but, once it tastes blood, it can survive off its host for only three to four days.

It was once thought that fleas spend most of their lives in the environment, but we now know that fleas won't willingly jump off a dog unless leaping to another dog or when physically removed by brushing, bathing or other manipulation. Flea eggs, on the other hand, are shiny and smooth, and they roll off the animal and into the environment. The eggs, larvae and pupae then exist in the environment, but once the adult finds a susceptible animal, it's home sweet home until the flea is forced to seek refuge elsewhere.

Since adult fleas live on the animal and immature forms survive in the environment, a successful treatment plan must address all stages of the flea life cycle. There are now several safe and effective flea-control products that can be applied on a monthly

FLEA PREVENTION FOR YOUR DOG

- Discuss with your veterinarian the safest product to protect your dog, likely in the form of a monthly tablet or a liquid preparation placed on the back of the dog's neck.
- For dogs suffering from flea-bite dermatitis, a shampoo or topical insecticide treatment is required.
- Your lawn and property should be sprayed with an insecticide designed to kill fleas and ticks that lurk outdoors.
- Using a flea comb, check the dog's coat regularly for any signs of parasites.
- Practice good housekeeping. Vacuum floors, carpets and furniture regularly, especially in the areas that the dog frequents, and wash the dog's bedding weekly.
- Follow up house-cleaning with carpet shampoos and sprays to rid the house of fleas at all stages of development. Insect growth regulators are the safest option.

basis. These include fipronil, imidacloprid, selamectin and permethrin (found in several formulations). Most of these products have significant flea-killing rates within 24 hours. However, none of them will control the immature forms in the environment. To accomplish this, there are a variety of insect growth regulators that can be sprayed into

THE FLEA'S LIFE CYCLE

What came first, the flea or the egg? This age-old mystery is more difficult to comprehend than the  actual cycle of the flea. Fleas usually live only about four months. A female can lay 2,000 eggs in her lifetime.

Egg

After ten days of rolling around your carpet or under your furniture, the eggs hatch into larvae, which feed on various and sundry debris. In days or

Larva

months, depending on the climate, the larvae spin cocoons and develop into the pupal or nymph stage, which quickly develop into fleas.

Pupa

These immature fleas must locate a host within 10 to 14 days or they will die. Only about 1% of the flea population exist as adult fleas, while the other 99% exist as eggs, larvae or pupae.

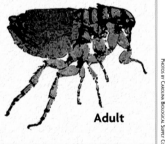

Adult

PHOTOS BY CAROLINA BIOLOGICAL SUPPLY CO.

KILL FLEAS THE NATURAL WAY

If you choose not to go the route of conventional medication, there are some natural ways to ward off fleas:

- Dust your dog with a natural flea powder, composed of such herbal goodies as rosemary, wormwood, pennyroyal, citronella, rue, tobacco powder and eucalyptus.
- Apply diatomaceous earth, the fossilized remains of single-cell algae, to your carpets, furniture and pet's bedding. Even though it's not good for dogs, it's even worse for fleas, which will dry up swiftly and die.
- Brush your dog frequently, give him adequate exercise and let him fast occasionally. All of these activities strengthen the dog's system and make him more resistant to disease and parasites.
- Bathe your dog with a capful of pennyroyal or eucalyptus oil.
- Feed a natural diet, free of additives and preservatives. Add some fresh garlic and brewer's yeast to the dog's morning portion, as these items have flea-repelling properties.

the environment (e.g., pyriprox-yfen, methoprene, fenoxycarb) as well as insect development inhibitors such as lufenuron that can be administered. These compounds have no effect on adult fleas, but they stop imma-ture forms from developing into

adults. In years gone by we relied heavily on toxic insecticides (such as organophosphates, organochlo-rines and carbamates) to manage the flea problem, but today's options are not only much safer to use on our pets but also safer for the environment.

TICKS

Ticks are members of the spider class (arachnids) and are blood-sucking parasites capable of transmitting a variety of diseases, including Lyme disease, ehrlichiosis, babesiosis and Rocky Mountain spotted fever. It's easy to see ticks on your own skin, but it is more of a challenge when your Chow Chow is affected. Whenever you happen to be planning a stroll in a tick-infested area (especially forests, grassy or wooded areas or parks) be prepared to do a thorough inspection of your dog afterward to search for ticks. Ticks can be tricky, so make sure you spend time looking in the ears, between the toes and everywhere else where a tick might hide. Ticks need to be attached for 24–72 hours before they transmit most of the diseases that they carry, so you do have a window of opportunity for some preventive intervention.

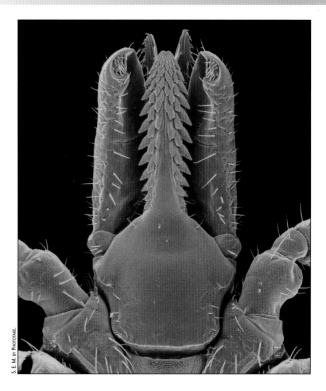

S. E. M. BY PHOTOTAKE.

A TICKING BOMB

There is nothing good about a tick's harpooning his nose into your dog's skin. Among the diseases caused by ticks are Rocky Mountain spotted fever, canine ehrlichiosis, canine babesiosis, canine hepatozoonosis and Lyme disease. If a dog is allergic to the saliva of a female wood tick, he can develop tick paralysis.

Female ticks live to eat and breed. They can lay between 4,000 and 5,000 eggs and they die soon after. Males, on the other hand, live only to mate with the females and continue the process as long as they are able. Most ticks live on multiple hosts before parasitizing dogs. The immature forms typically reside on grass and shrubs, waiting for susceptible animals to walk by. The larvae and nymph stages typically feed on wildlife.

If only a few ticks are present on a dog, they can be plucked out, but it is important to remove the entire head and mouthparts,

A scanning electron micrograph of the head of a female deer tick, *Ixodes dammini,* a parasitic tick that carries Lyme disease.

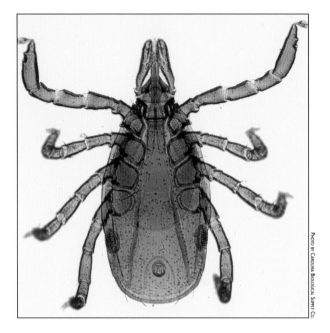

Photo by Carolina Biological Supply Co.

Deer tick,
Ixodes dammini.

which may be deeply embedded in the skin. This is best accomplished with forceps designed especially for this purpose; fingers can be used but should be protected with rubber gloves, plastic wrap or at least a paper towel. The tick should be grasped as closely as possible to the animal's skin and should be pulled upward with steady, even pressure. Do not squeeze, crush or puncture the body of the tick or you risk exposure to any disease carried by that tick. Once the ticks have been removed, the sites of attachment should be disinfected. Your hands should then be washed with soap and water to further minimize risk of contagion. The tick should be disposed of in a container of alcohol or household bleach.

Some of the newer flea products, specifically those with fipronil, selamectin and permethrin, have effect against some, but not all, species of tick. Flea collars containing appropriate pesticides (e.g., propoxur, chlorfenvinphos) can aid in tick control. In most areas, such collars should be placed on animals in March, at the beginning of the tick season, and changed regularly. Leaving the collar on when the pesticide level is waning invites the development of resistance. Amitraz collars are also good for tick control, and the active ingredient does not interfere with other flea-control products. The ingredient helps prevent the attachment of ticks to the skin and will cause those ticks already on the skin to detach themselves.

TICK CONTROL

Removal of underbrush and leaf litter and the thinning of trees in areas where tick control is desired are recommended. These actions remove the cover and food sources for small animals that serve as hosts for ticks. With continued mowing of grasses in these areas, the probability of ticks' surviving is further reduced. A variety of insecticide ingredients (e.g., resmethrin, carbaryl, permethrin, chlorpyrifos, dioxathion and allethrin) are registered for tick control around the home.

MITES

Mites are tiny arachnid parasites that parasitize the skin of dogs. Skin diseases caused by mites are referred to as "mange," and there are many different forms seen in dogs. These forms are very different from one another, each one warranting an individual description.

Sarcoptic mange, or scabies, is one of the itchiest conditions that affects dogs. The microscopic *Sarcoptes* mites burrow into the superficial layers of the skin and can drive dogs crazy with itchiness. They are also communicable to people, although they can't complete their reproductive cycle on people. In addition to being tiny, the mites also are often difficult to find when trying to make a diagnosis. Skin scrapings from multiple areas are examined microscopically but, even then, sometimes the mites cannot be found.

Fortunately, scabies is relatively easy to treat, and there are a variety of products that will successfully kill the mites. Since the mites can't live in the environment for very long without feeding, a complete cure is usually possible within four to eight weeks.

Cheyletiellosis is caused by a relatively large mite, which sometimes can be seen even without a microscope. Often referred to as "walking dandruff," this also causes itching, but not usually as profound as with scabies. While *Cheyletiella* mites can survive somewhat longer

PHOTO BY PHOTOTAKE.

Sarcoptes scabiei, commonly known as the "itch mite."

in the environment than scabies mites, they too are relatively easy to treat, being responsive to not only the medications used to treat scabies but also often to flea-control products.

Otodectes cynotis is the canine ear mite and is one of the more common causes of mange, especially in young dogs in shelters or pet stores. That's because the mites are typically present in large numbers and are quickly spread to nearby animals. The mites rarely do much harm but can be difficult

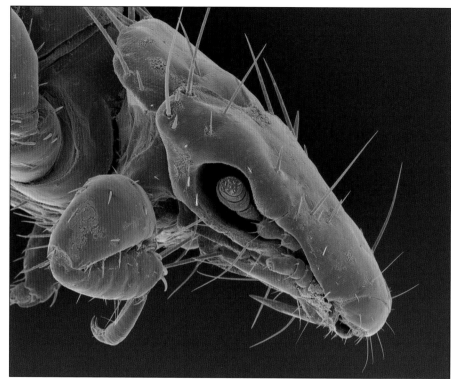

Micrograph of a dog louse, *Heterodoxus spiniger*. Female lice attach their eggs to the hairs of the dog. As the eggs hatch, the larval lice bite and feed on the blood. Lice can also feed on dead skin and hair. This feeding activity can cause hair loss and skin problems.

S. E. M. BY DR. DENNIS KUNKEL, UNIVERSITY OF HAWAII

to eradicate if the treatment regimen is not comprehensive. While many try to treat the condition with ear drops only, this is the most common cause of treatment failure. Ear drops cause the mites to simply move out of the ears and as far away as possible (usually to the base of the tail) until the insecticide levels in the ears drop to an acceptable level—then it's back to business as usual! The successful treatment of ear mites requires treating all animals in the household with a systemic insecticide, such as selamectin, or a combination of miticidal ear drops combined with whole-body flea-control preparations.

Demodicosis, sometimes referred to as red mange, can be one of the most difficult forms of mange to treat. Part of the problem has to do with the fact that the mites live in the hair follicles and they are relatively well shielded from topical and systemic products. The main issue, however, is that demodectic mange typically results only when there is some underlying process interfering with the dog's immune system.

Since *Demodex* mites are normal residents of the skin of

mammals, including humans, there is usually a mite population explosion only when the immune system fails to keep the number of mites in check. In young animals, the immune deficit may be transient or may reflect an actual inherited immune problem. In older animals, demodicosis is usually seen only when there is another disease hampering the immune system, such as diabetes, cancer, thyroid problems or the use of immune-suppressing drugs. Accordingly, treatment involves not only trying to kill the mange mites but also discerning what is interfering with immune function and correcting it if possible.

Chiggers represent several different species of mite that don't parasitize dogs specifically, but do latch on to passersby and can cause irritation. The problem is most prevalent in wooded areas in the late summer and fall. Treatment is not difficult, as the mites do not complete their life cycle on dogs and are susceptible to a variety of miticidal products.

MOSQUITOES

Mosquitoes have long been known to transmit a variety of diseases to people, as well as just being biting pests during warm weather. They also pose a real risk to pets. Not only do they carry deadly heart-

ILLUSTRATION BY PHOTOTAKE

worms but recently there also has been much concern over their involvement with West Nile virus. While we can avoid heartworm with the use of preventive medications, there are no such preventives for West Nile virus. The only method of prevention in endemic areas is active mosquito control. Fortunately, most dogs that have been exposed to the virus only developed flu-like symptoms and, to date, there have not been the large number of reported deaths in canines as seen in some other species.

Illustration of *Demodex folliculoram.*

MOSQUITO REPELLENT

Low concentrations of DEET (less than 10%), found in many human mosquito repellents, have been safely used in dogs but, in these concentrations, probably give only about two hours of protection. DEET may be safe in these small concentrations, but since it is not licensed for use on dogs, there is no research proving its safety for dogs. Products containing permethrin give the longest-lasting protection, perhaps two to four weeks. As DEET is not licensed for use on dogs, and both DEET and permethrin can be quite toxic to cats, appropriate care should be exercised. Other products, such as those containing oil of citronella, also have some mosquito-repellent activity, but typically have a relatively short duration of action.

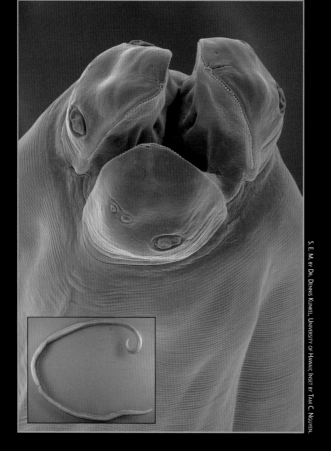

The ascarid roundworm *Toxocara canis*, showing the mouth with three lips. Inset: Photomicrograph of the roundworm *Ascaris lumbricoides.*

ASCARID DANGERS

The most commonly encountered worms in dogs are roundworms known as ascarids. *Toxascaris leonine* and *Toxocara canis* are the two species that infect dogs. Subsisting in the dog's stomach and intestines, adult round-worms can grow to 7 inches in length and adult females can lay in excess of 200,000 eggs in a single day.

In humans, visceral larval migrans affects people who have ingested eggs of *Toxocara canis*, which frequently contaminates children's sandboxes, beaches and park grounds. The round-worms reside in the human's stomach and intestines, as they would in a dog's, but do not mature. Instead, they find their way to the liver, lungs and skin, or even to the heart or kidneys in severe cases. Deworming puppies is critical in preventing the infection in humans, and young children should never handle nursing pups who have not been dewormed.

INTERNAL PARASITES: WORMS

ASCARIDS

Ascarids are intestinal round-worms that rarely cause severe disease in dogs. Nonetheless, they are of major public health signifi-cance because they can be trans-ferred to people. Sadly, it is chil-dren who are most commonly affected by the parasite, probably from inadvertently ingesting ascarid-contaminated soil. In fact, many yards and children's sand-boxes contain appreciable numbers of ascarid eggs. So, while ascarids don't bite dogs or latch onto their intestines to suck blood, they do cause some nasty medical conditions in children and are best eradicated from our furry friends. Because pups can start passing ascarid eggs by three weeks of age, most parasite-control programs begin at two weeks of age and are repeated every two weeks until pups are eight weeks old. It is important to

HOOKED ON ANCYLOSTOMA

Adult dogs can become infected by the bloodsucking nematodes we commonly call hookworms via ingesting larvae from the ground or via the larvae penetrating the dog's skin. It is not uncommon for infected dogs to show no symptoms of hookworm infestation. Sometimes symptoms occur within ten days of exposure. These symptoms can include bloody diarrhea, anemia, loss of weight and general weakness. Dogs pass the hookworm eggs in their stools, which serves as the vet's method of identifying the infestation. The hookworm larvae can encyst themselves in the dog's tissues and be released when the dog is experiencing stress.

Caused by an *Ancylostoma* species whose common host is the dog, cutaneous larval migrans affects humans, causing itching and lumps and streaks beneath the surface of the skin.

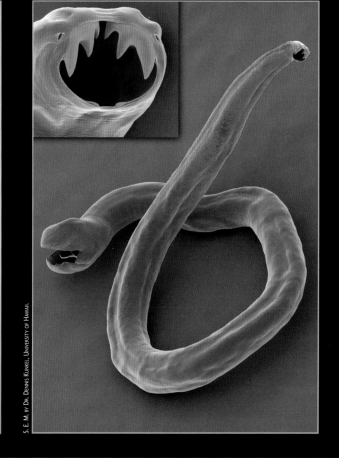

realize that bitches can pass ascarids to their pups even if they test negative prior to whelping. Accordingly, bitches are best treated at the same time as the pups.

HOOKWORMS

Unlike ascarids, hookworms do latch onto a dog's intestinal tract and can cause significant loss of blood and protein. Similar to ascarids, hookworms can be transmitted to humans, where they cause a condition known as cutaneous larval migrans. Dogs can become infected either by consuming the infective larvae or by the larvae's penetrating the skin directly. People most often get infected when they are lying on the ground (such as on a beach) and the larvae penetrate the skin. Yes, the larvae can penetrate through a beach blanket. Hookworms are typically susceptible to the same medications used to treat ascarids.

The hookworm *Ancylostoma caninum* infests the intestines of dogs. Inset: Note the row of hooks at the posterior end, used to anchor the worm to the intestinal wall.

WHIPWORMS

Whipworms latch onto the lower aspects of the dog's colon and can cause cramping and diarrhea. Eggs do not start to appear in the dog's feces until about three months after the dog was infected. This worm has a peculiar life cycle, which makes it more difficult to control than ascarids or hookworms. The good thing is that whipworms rarely are transferred to people.

Some of the medications used to treat ascarids and hookworms are also effective against whipworms, but, in general, a separate treatment protocol is needed. Since most of the medications are effective against the adults but not the eggs or larvae, treatment is typically repeated in three weeks, and then often in three

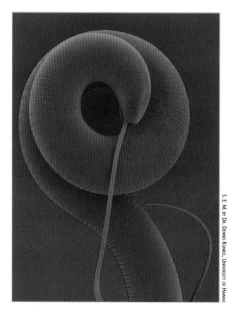

Adult whipworm, *Trichuris* sp., an intestinal parasite.

S. E. M. BY DR. DENNIS KUNKEL, UNIVERSITY OF HAWAII.

WORM-CONTROL GUIDELINES

- Practice sanitary habits with your dog and home.
- Clean up after your dog and don't let him sniff or eat other dogs' droppings.
- Control insects and fleas in the dog's environment. Fleas, lice, cockroaches, beetles, mice and rats can act as hosts for various worms.
- Prevent dogs from eating uncooked meat, raw poultry and dead animals.
- Keep dogs and children from playing in sand and soil.
- Kennel dogs on cement or gravel; avoid dirt runs.
- Administer heartworm preventatives regularly.
- Have your vet examine your dog's stools at your annual visits.
- Select a boarding kennel carefully so as to avoid contamination from other dogs or an unsanitary environment.
- Prevent dogs from roaming. Obey local leash laws.

months as well. Unfortunately, since dogs don't develop resistance to whipworms, it is difficult to prevent them from getting reinfected if they visit soil contaminated with whipworm eggs.

TAPEWORMS

There are many different species of tapeworm that affect dogs, but *Dipylidium caninum* is probably the most common and is spread by fleas. Flea larvae feed on organic debris and tapeworm eggs in the environment and, when a dog chews at himself and manages to ingest fleas, he might get a dose of tapeworm at the same time. The tapeworm then develops further in the intestine of the dog.

The tapeworm itself, which latches onto the intestinal wall, is composed of numerous segments. When the segments break off into the intestine (as proglottids), they may accumulate around the rectum, like grains of rice. While this tapeworm is disgusting in its behavior, it is not directly communicable to humans (although humans can also get infected by swallowing fleas).

A much more dangerous flatworm is *Echinococcus multilocularis*, which is typically found in foxes, coyotes and wolves. The eggs are passed in the feces and infect rodents, and, when dogs eat the rodents, the dogs can be infected by thousands of adult tapeworms. While the parasites don't cause many problems in dogs, this is considered the most lethal worm infection that people can get. Take appropriate precautions if you live in an area in which these tapeworms are found. Do not use mulch that may contain feces of dogs, cats or wildlife, and discourage your pets from hunting

wildlife. Treat these tapeworm infections aggressively in pets, because if humans get infected, approximately half die.

HEARTWORMS

Heartworm disease is caused by the parasite *Dirofilaria immitis* and is seen in dogs around the world. A member of the roundworm group, it is spread between dogs by the bite of an infected mosquito. The mosquito injects infective larvae into the dog's skin with its bite, and these larvae develop under the skin for a period of time before making their way to the heart. There they develop into adults, which grow and create blockages of the heart, lungs and major blood vessels there. They also start producing offspring (microfilariae)

S. E. M. BY DR. DENNIS KUNKEL, UNIVERSITY OF HAWAII.

A dog tapeworm proglottid (body segment).

S. E. M. BY DR. DENNIS KUNKEL, UNIVERSITY OF HAWAII.

The dog tapeworm *Taenia pisiformis*.

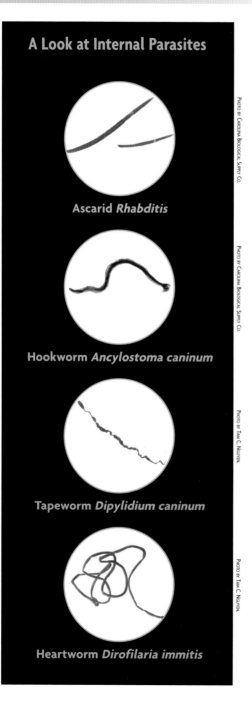

A Look at Internal Parasites

Ascarid *Rhabditis*

Hookworm *Ancylostoma caninum*

Tapeworm *Dipylidium caninum*

Heartworm *Dirofilaria immitis*

and these microfilariae circulate in the bloodstream, waiting to hitch a ride when the next mosquito bites. Once in the mosquito, the microfilariae develop into infective larvae and the entire process is repeated.

When dogs get infected with heartworm, over time they tend to develop symptoms associated with heart disease, such as coughing, exercise intolerance and potentially many other manifestations. Diagnosis is confirmed by either seeing the microfilariae themselves in blood samples or using immunologic tests (antigen testing) to identify the presence of adult heartworms. Since antigen tests measure the presence of adult heartworms and microfilarial tests measure offspring produced by adults, neither are positive until six to seven months after the initial infection. However, the beginning of damage can occur by fifth-stage larvae as early as three months after infection. Thus it is possible for dogs to be harboring problem-causing larvae for up to three months before either type of test would identify an infection.

The good news is that there are great protocols available for preventing heartworm in dogs. Testing is critical in the process, and it is important to understand the benefits as well as the limitations of such testing. All dogs six months of age or older that have not been on continuous heartworm-preventive medication

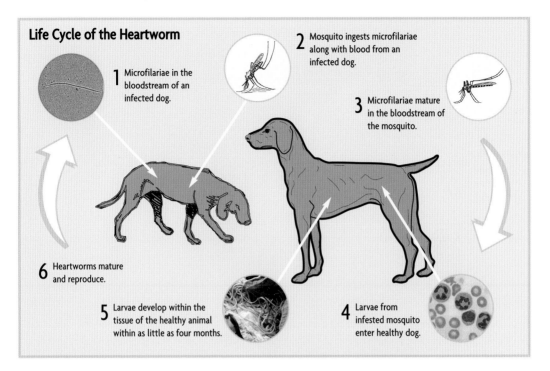

Life Cycle of the Heartworm

1 Microfilariae in the bloodstream of an infected dog.

2 Mosquito ingests microfilariae along with blood from an infected dog.

3 Microfilariae mature in the bloodstream of the mosquito.

6 Heartworms mature and reproduce.

5 Larvae develop within the tissue of the healthy animal within as little as four months.

4 Larvae from infested mosquito enter healthy dog.

should be screened with microfilarial or antigen tests. For dogs receiving preventive medication, periodic antigen testing helps assess the effectiveness of the preventives. The American Heartworm Society guidelines suggest that annual retesting may not be necessary when owners have absolutely provided continuous heartworm prevention. Retesting on a two- to three-year interval may be sufficient in these cases. However, your veterinarian will likely have specific guidelines under which heartworm preventives will be prescribed, and many prefer to err on the side of safety and retest annually.

It is indeed fortunate that heartworm is relatively easy to prevent, because treatments can be as life-threatening as the disease itself. Treatment requires a two-step process that kills the adult heartworms first and then the microfilariae. Prevention is obviously preferable; this involves a once-monthly oral or topical treatment. The most common oral preventives include ivermectin (not suitable for some breeds), moxidectin and milbemycin oxime; the once-a-month topical drug selamectin provides heartworm protection in addition to flea, tick and other parasite controls.

From coast to coast, Chows are popular show dogs. In the West you may meet one of the sensational Chows bred by George and Kathy Beliew of California.

CHOW CHOW

Is dog showing in your blood? Are you excited by the idea of gaiting your handsome Chow around the ring to the thunderous applause of an enthusiastic audience? Are you certain that your beloved Chow is flawless? You are not alone! Every loving owner thinks that his dog has no faults, or too few to mention. No matter how many times an owner reads the breed standard, he cannot find any faults in his aristocratic companion dog. If this sounds like you, and if you are considering entering your Chow in a dog show, here are some basic questions to ask yourself:

- Did you purchase a "show-quality" puppy from the breeder?
- Is your puppy at least six months of age?
- Does the puppy exhibit correct show type for his breed?
- Does your puppy have any disqualifying faults?
- Is your Chow registered with the American Kennel Club?
- How much time do you have to devote to training, grooming, conditioning and exhibiting your dog?

- Do you understand the rules and regulations of a dog show?
- Do you have time to learn how to show your dog properly?
- Do you have the financial resources to invest in showing your dog?
- Will you show the dog yourself or hire a professional handler?

MEET THE AKC
The American Kennel Club is the main governing body of the dog sport in the United States. Founded in 1884, the AKC consists of 500 or more independent dog clubs plus 4,500 affiliated clubs, all of which follow the AKC rules and regulations. Additionally, the AKC maintains a registry for pure-bred dogs in the US and works to preserve the integrity of the sport and its continuation in the country. Over 1,000,000 dogs are registered each year, representing about 150 recognized breeds. There are over 15,000 competitive events held annually for which over 2,000,000 dogs enter to participate. Dogs compete to earn over 40 different titles, from champion to Companion Dog to Master Agility Champion.

BEST OF WINNERS & OPPOSITE

If you have acquired your Chow puppy from a top breeder, your chances of shining in the ring are happily increased. Owner, Karen Tracy.

your way up" part that you must keep in mind.

Assuming that you have purchased a puppy of the correct type and quality for showing, let's begin to examine the world of showing and what's required to get started. Although the entry fee into a dog show is nominal, there are lots of other hidden costs involved with "finishing" your Chow, that is, making him a champion. Things like equipment, travel, training and conditioning all cost money. A more serious campaign will include fees for a professional handler, boarding, cross-country travel and advertising. Top-winning show dogs can represent a very considerable investment—over $100,000 has been spent in campaigning some dogs. (The investment can be less, of course, for owners who don't use professional handlers.)

Many owners, on the other hand, enter their "average" Chows in dog shows for the fun and enjoyment of it. Dog showing makes an absorbing hobby, with many rewards for dogs and

• Do you have a vehicle that can accommodate your weekend trips to the dog shows?

Success in the show ring requires more than a pretty face, a waggy tail and a pocketful of liver. Even though dog shows can be exciting and enjoyable, the sport of conformation makes great demands on the exhibitors and the dogs. Winning exhibitors live for their dogs, devoting time and money to their dogs' presentation, conditioning and training. Very few novices, even those with good dogs, will find themselves in the winners' circle, though it does happen. Don't be disheartened, though. Every exhibitor began as a novice and worked his way up to the Group ring. It's the "working

AKC GROUPS

For showing purposes, the American Kennel Club divides its recognized breeds into seven groups: Sporting Dogs, Hounds, Working Dogs, Terriers, Toys, Non-Sporting Dogs and Herding Dogs. The Chow Chow competes in the Non-Sporting Group.

a lifetime; it's certainly much better than a deer tick! Soon you will be envisioning yourself in the center ring at the Westminster Kennel Club Dog Show in New York City, competing for the prestigious Best in Show cup. This magical dog show is televised annually from Madison Square Garden, and the victorious dog becomes a celebrity overnight.

AKC CONFORMATION SHOWING

GETTING STARTED

Visiting a dog show as a spectator is a great place to start. Pick up

owners alike. If you're having fun, meeting other people who share your interests and enjoying the overall experience, you likely will catch the "bug." Once the dog-show bug bites, its effects can last

Placing at the Westminster Kennel Club dog show is a Smooth owned by Karen Tracy.

DRESS THE PART

It's a dog show, so don't forget your costume. Even though the show is about the dog, you also must play your role well. You have been cast as the "dog handler" and you must smartly dress the part. Solid colors make a nice complement to the dog's coat, but choose colors that contrast. You don't want to be wearing a solid color that blends mostly or entirely with the major or only color of your dog. Whether the show is indoors or out, you still must dress properly. You want the judge to perceive you as being professional, so polish, polish, polish! And don't forget to wear sensible shoes; remember, you have to gait around the ring with your dog.

Here's breeder-judge Dr. Sam Draper awarding a handsome Chow at the Morris and Essex show. Owner, Karen Tracy.

the show catalog to find out what time your breed is being shown, who is judging the breed and in which ring the classes will be held. To start, Chows compete against other Chows, and the winner is selected as Best of Breed by the judge. This is the procedure for each breed. At a group show, all of the Best of Breed winners go on to compete for Group One in their respective group. For example, all Best of Breed winners in a given group compete against each other; this is done for all seven groups. Finally, all seven group winners go head to head in the ring for the Best in Show award.

What most spectators don't understand is the basic idea of conformation. A dog show is often referred as a "conformation" show. This means that the judge should decide how each dog stacks up (conforms) to the breed standard for his given breed: how well does this Chow conform to the ideal representative detailed in the standard? Ideally, this is what happens. In reality, however, this ideal often gets slighted as the judge compares Chow #1 to Chow #2. Again, the ideal is that each dog is judged based on his merits in comparison to his breed standard, not in comparison to the other dogs in the ring. It is easier for judges to compare dogs of the same breed to decide which they think is the better specimen; in the Group and Best in Show ring, however, it is very difficult to compare one breed to another, like apples to oranges. Thus the dog's conformation to the breed standard—not to mention advertising dollars and good handling—is essential to success in conformation shows. The dog described in the standard (the standard for each AKC breed is written and approved by the breed's national parent club and then submitted to the AKC for approval) is the perfect dog of that breed, and breeders keep their eye on the standard when they choose which dogs to breed, hoping to get closer and closer to the ideal with each litter.

Another good first step for the novice is to join a dog club. You will be astonished by the many and different kinds of dog clubs in the country, with about 5,000 clubs holding events every year. Most clubs require that prospective new members present two letters of recommendation from existing members. Perhaps you've made some friends visiting a show held by a particular club and you would like to join that club. Dog clubs may specialize in a single breed, like a local or regional Chow club, or in a specific pursuit, such as obedience, tracking or hunting tests. There are all-breed clubs for all-dog enthusiasts; they sponsor special training days, seminars on topics like grooming or handling or lectures on breeding or canine genetics. There are also clubs that specialize in certain types of dogs, like herding dogs, hunting dogs, companion dogs, etc.

A parent club is the national organization, sanctioned by the AKC, which promotes and safeguards its breed in the country. The Chow Chow Club was formed in 1906 and can be contacted on the Internet at www.chowclub.org. The parent club holds an annual national specialty show, usually in a different city each year, in which many of the country's top dogs, handlers and breeders gather to compete. At a specialty show, only members of a single breed are invited to participate. There are also Group specialties, in which all members of a Group are

In recent times Chows are strong contenders for Best in Show, as this Chow owned by Kathy Beliew effortlessly demonstrates.

Although Smooths aren't as popular at shows as Roughs, there are many exceptional ones in the ring. Owner, Karen Tracy.

invited. For more information about dog clubs in your area, contact the AKC at www.akc.org on the Internet or write them at their Raleigh, NC address.

How Shows Are Organized

Three kinds of conformation shows are offered by the AKC. There is the all-breed show, in which all AKC-recognized breeds can compete; the specialty show, which is for one breed only and usually sponsored by the breed's parent club and the group show, for all breeds in one of the seven AKC groups. The Chow competes in the Non-Sporting Group.

For a dog to become an AKC champion of record, the dog must earn 15 points at shows. The points must be awarded by at least three different judges and must include two "majors" under different judges. A "major" is a three-, four- or five-point win, and the number of points per win is determined by the number of dogs competing in the show on that day. (Dogs that are absent or are excused are not counted.) The number of points that are awarded varies from breed to breed. More dogs are needed to attain a major in more popular breeds, and fewer dogs are needed in less popular breeds. Yearly, the AKC evaluates the number of dogs in competition in each division (there are 14 divisions in all, based on geogra-

FIVE CLASSES AT SHOWS

At most AKC all-breed shows, there are five regular classes offered: Puppy, Novice, Bred-by-Exhibitor, American-bred and Open. The Puppy Class is usually divided as 6 to 9 months of age and 9 to 12 months of age. When deciding in which class to enter your dog, whether male or female, you must carefully check the show schedule to make sure that you have selected the right class. Depending on the age of the dog, its previous first-place wins and the sex of the dog, you must make the best choice. It is possible to enter a one-year-old dog who has not won sufficient first places in any of the non-Puppy Classes, though the competition is more intense the further you progress from the Puppy Class.

phy) and may or may not change the numbers of dogs required for each number of points. For example, a major in Division 2 (Delaware, New Jersey and Pennsylvania) recently required 17 dogs or 16 bitches for a three-point major, 29 dogs or 27 bitches for a four-point major and 51 dogs or 46 bitches for a five-point major. The Chow attracts numerically proportionate representation at all-breed shows.

Only one dog and one bitch of each breed can win points at a given show. There are no "co-ed" classes except for champions of record. Dogs and bitches do not compete against each other until they are champions. Dogs that are not champions (referred to as "class dogs") compete in one of five classes. The class in which a dog is entered depends on age and previous show wins. First there is the Puppy Class (sometimes divided further into classes for 6- to 9-month-olds and 9- to 12-month-olds); next is the Novice Class (for dogs that have no points toward their championship and whose only first-place wins have come in the Puppy Class or the Novice Class, the latter class limited to three first places); then there is the American-bred Class (for dogs bred in the US); the Bred-by-Exhibitor Class (for dogs handled by their breeders or by immediate family members of their breeders) and the Open Class

SHOW POTENTIAL

How possible is it to predict how your ten-week-old puppy will eventually do in the show ring? Most show dogs reach their prime at around three years of age, when their bodies are physically mature and their coats are in "full bloom." Experienced breeders, having watched countless pups grow into Best of Breed winners, recognize the glowing attributes that spell "show potential." When selecting a puppy for show, it's best to trust the breeder to recommend which puppy will best suit your aspirations. Some breeders recommend starting with a male puppy, which likely will be more "typey" than his female counterpart.

(for any non-champions). Any dog may enter the Open class, regardless of age or win history, but to be competitive the dog should be older and have ring experience.

The judge at the show begins judging the male dogs in the Puppy Class(es) and proceeds through the other classes. The judge awards first through fourth place in each class. The first-place winners of each class then compete with one another in the Winners Class to determine Winners Dog. The judge then starts over with the bitches, beginning with the Puppy Class(es) and proceeding up to the Winners Class to award Winners Bitch, just as he did with the dogs. A Reserve Winners Dog and Reserve

AMERICAN KENNEL CLUB TITLES

The AKC offers over 40 different titles to dogs in competition. Depending on the events that your dog can enter, different titles apply. Some titles can be applied as prefixes, meaning that they are placed before the dog's name (e.g., Ch. King of the Road) and others are used as suffixes, placed after the dog's name (e.g., King of the Road, CD).

These titles are used as prefixes:

Conformation Dog Shows
- Ch. (Champion)

Obedience Trials
- NOC (National Obedience Champion)
- OTCH (Obedience Trial Champion)
- VCCH (Versatile Companion Champion)

Tracking Tests
- CT [Champion Tracker (TD,TDX and VST)]

Agility Trials
- MACH (Master Agility Champion)
- MACH2, MACH3, MACH4, etc.

Field Trials
- FC (Field Champion)
- AFC (Amateur Field Champion)
- NFC (National Field Champion)
- NAFC (National Amateur Field Champion)
- NOGDC (National Open Gun Dog Champion)
- AKC GDSC (AKC Gun Dog Stake Champion)
- AKC RGDSC (AKC Retrieving Gun Dog Stake Champion)

Herding Trials
- HC (Herding Champion)

Dual
- DC (Dual Champion — Ch. and FC)

Triple
- TC (Triple Champion — Ch., FC and OTCH)

Coonhounds
- NCH (Nite Champion)
- GNCH (Grand Nite Champion)
- SGNCH (Senior Grand Nite Champion)
- SGCH (Senior Grand Champion)
- GFC (Grand Field Champion)
- SGFC (Senior Grand Field Champion)
- WCH (Water Race Champion)
- GWCH (Water Race Grand Champion)
- SGWCH (Senior Grand Water Race Champion)

These titles are used as suffixes:

Obedience
- CD (Companion Dog)
- CDX (Companion Dog Excellent)
- UD (Utility Dog)
- UDX (Utility Dog Excellent)
- VCD1 (Versatile Companion Dog 1)
- VCD2 (Versatile Companion Dog 2)
- VCD3 (Versatile Companion Dog 3)
- VCD4 (Versatile Companion Dog 4)

Tracking Tests
- TD (Tracking Dog)
- TDX (Tracking Dog Excellent)
- VST (Variable Surface Tracker)

Agility Trials*
- NA (Novice Agility)
- OA (Open Agility)
- AX (Agility Excellent)
- MX (Master Agility Excellent)
- NAJ (Novice Jumpers with weaves)
- OAJ (Open Jumpers with weaves)
- AXJ (Excellent Jumpers with weaves)
- MXJ (Master Excellent Jumpers with weaves)

Hunting Test
- JH (Junior Hunter)
- SH (Senior Hunter)
- MH (Master Hunter)

Herding Test
- HT (Herding Tested)
- PT (Pre-Trial Tested)
- HS (Herding Started)
- HI (Herding Intermediate)
- HX (Herding Excellent)

Lure Coursing
- JC (Junior Courser)
- SC (Senior Courser)
- MC (Master Courser)

Earthdog
- JE (Junior Earthdog)
- SE (Senior Earthdog)
- ME (Master Earthdog)

*All titles also offered in Preferred Classes

Winners Bitch are also selected; they could be awarded the points in the case of a disqualification.

The Winners Dog and Winners Bitch are the two that are awarded the points for their breed. They then go on to compete with any champions of record (often called "specials") of their breed that are entered in the show. The champions may be dogs or bitches; in this class, all are shown together. The judge reviews the Winners Dog and Winners Bitch along with all of the champions to select the Best of Breed winner. The Best of Winners is selected between the Winners Dog and Winners Bitch; if one of these two is selected Best of Breed as well, he or she is automatically determined Best of Winners. Lastly, the judge selects Best of Opposite Sex to the Best of Breed winner. The Best of Breed winner then goes on to the Group competition.

At a Group or all-breed show, the Best of Breed winners from each breed are divided into their respective groups to compete against one another for Group One through Group Four. Group One (first place) is awarded to the dog that best lives up to the ideal for his breed as described in the standard. A Group judge, therefore, must have a thorough working knowledge of many breed standards. After placements have been made in each Group, the seven Group One winners (from the

Sporting Group, Toy Group, Hound Group, etc.) compete against each other for the top honor, Best in Show.

There are different ways to find out about dog shows in your area. The American Kennel Club's monthly magazine, the *American Kennel Gazette,* is accompanied by the *Events Calendar;* this magazine is available through subscription. You can also look on the AKC's and your parent club's websites for information and check the event listings in your local newspaper.

Your Chow must be six months of age or older and regis-

JUNIOR SHOWMANSHIP

For budding dog handlers, ages 10 to 18 years, Junior Showmanship competitions are an excellent training ground for the next generation of dog professionals. Owning and caring for a dog are wonderful methods of teaching children responsibility, and Junior Showmanship builds upon that foundation. Juniors learn by grooming, handling and training their dogs, and the quality of a junior's presentation of the dog (and himself) is evaluated by a licensed judge. The junior can enter with any registered AKC dog to compete, including an Indefinite Listing Privilege, provided that the dog lives with him or a member of his family.

tered with the AKC in order to be entered in AKC-sanctioned shows in which there are classes for the Chow. Your Chow also must not possess any disqualifying faults and must be sexually intact. The reason for the latter is simple: dog shows are the proving grounds to determine which dogs and bitches are worthy of being bred. If they cannot be bred, that defeats the purpose! On that note, only dogs that have achieved championships, thus proving their excellent quality, should be bred. If you have spayed or neutered your dog, however, there are many AKC events other than conformation, such as obedience trials, agility

This handsome Chow Chow, winning Best of Breed, is owned by Karen Tracy.

trials and the Canine Good Citizen® program, in which you and your Chow can participate.

YOU'RE AT THE SHOW, NOW WHAT?
You will fill out an entry form when you register for the show. You must decide and designate on the form in which class you will enter your puppy or adult dog. Remember that some classes are more competitive than others and have limitations based on age and win history. Hopefully you will not be in the first class of the day, so you can take some time watching exactly how the judge is conducting the ring. Notice how the handlers are stacking their dogs, meaning setting them up. Does the judge prefer the dogs to be facing one direction or another? Take special note as to how the judge is moving the dogs and how he is instructing the handlers. Is he moving them up and back, once or twice around, in a triangle?

A Group 1 award presented by Dr. Samuel Draper to a Chow owned by Linda Albert.

If possible, you will want to get your number beforehand. Your assigned number must be attached as an armband or with a clip on your outer garment. Do not enter the ring without your number. The ring steward will usually call the exhibits in numerical order. If the exhibits are not called in order, you should strategically place your dog in the line. For instance, if your pup is small for his age, don't stand him next to a large entry; if your dog is reluctant to gait, get at the end of the line-up so that you don't interfere with the other dogs. The judge's first direction, usually, is for all of the handlers to "take the dogs around," which means that everyone gaits his dog around the periphery of the ring.

While you're in the ring, don't let yourself (or your dog) become distracted. Concentrate on your dog; he should have your full attention. Stack him in the best way possible. Teach him to free-stand while you hold a treat out for him. Let him understand that he must hold this position for at least a minute before you reward him. Follow the judge's instructions and be aware of what the judge is doing. Don't frustrate the judge by not paying attention to his directions.

When your dog's turn to be judged arrives, keep him steady and calm. The judge will inspect the dog's bite and dentition, overall musculature and structure and, in a male dog, the testicles, which must completely descend into the scrotum. Likewise, the judge will take note of the dog's alertness and temperament. Aggressiveness is a disqualification in most breeds, and so is shyness. A dog must always be approachable by the judge, even though aloofness is one of the breed's characteristics. Once the judge has completed his hands-on inspection, he will instruct you to gait the dog. A dog's gait indicates to the judge that the dog is correctly constructed. Each breed standard describes the ideal correct gait for that breed. After the judge has inspected all of the dogs in the class in this manner, he will ask the entire class to gait together. He will make his final selections after one last look over the class.

Whether you win or lose, the only one disappointed will be you. Never let your dog know that he's not "the winner." Most important is that you reaffirm your dog's love of the game. Reward him for behaving properly and for being the handsome boy or pretty girl that he or she is.

After your first or second experience in the ring, you will know what things you need to work on. Go home, practice and have fun with your Chow. With some time and effort, you and your well-trained show dog will soon be standing in the winners' circle with a blue ribbon!

Show breeders strive to produce correctly constructed Chows with friendly, reliable temperaments and proper coats. Owner, Linda Albert.

INDEX

*Page numbers in **boldface** indicate illustrations.*

𝔐𝔶 𝔆𝔥𝔬𝔴 𝔆𝔥𝔬𝔴

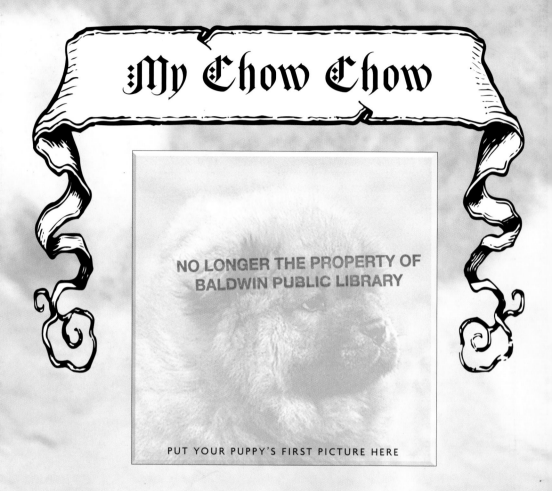

PUT YOUR PUPPY'S FIRST PICTURE HERE

Dog's Name _____

Date _____ Photographer _____